GASTRIC SLEEVE BARIATRIC COOKBOOK

Learn How to Keep The Weight Loss Post Operation, Fight The Food Addiction, and Take Care Of Your New Stomach with 200 Healthy Recipes, and A Delicious Meal Plan.

EVELYN PRICE

TABLE OF CONTENTS

CHAPTER 6

CHAPTER 8

INTRODUCTION

In recent years, the gastric sleeve has been one of the most used procedures for weight loss.

The "gastric sleeve" refers to a simple operation in which part of the stomach is removed and turned into a tube that limits food intake.

That said, in spite of its efficacy in terms of weight loss, not everyone who needs such an intervention can access it due to its high cost.

However, thanks to new advances in medicine which include robotic surgery and 3D printing, we hope this procedure will soon be more accessible to all those who need it.

Gastric sleeve is a method of reducing the size of the stomach that removes part of it. To achieve a hundred percent weight loss, other methods must be used as well.

The gastric sleeve has many benefits: It has the capacity to reduce the amount of food consumed by up to 30% as compared to before, it is easy to maintain and results can be seen right away.

In addition, one month after surgery, patients should have returned to eating normal amounts of food without gaining weight or experiencing any side effects.

For these reasons, gastric sleeve has become an extremely popular procedure for both men and women who wish to lose weight.

Among the people who choose to undergo surgery to achieve weight loss are both those who suffer from health problems associated with obesity and those who only wish to look better in their clothes.

The gastric sleeve is mainly used as a method of losing weight, but it is also used by those undergoing bariatric surgery.

This type of surgery focuses on patients who are at risk of developing serious illnesses due to their obesity, and thus must lose weight to prevent such illnesses from manifesting.

A good example would be diabetes: This illness occurs due to diet and lifestyle factors that lead to insulin resistance, which eventually causes diabetes.

A gastric sleeve could be used to prevent or treat diabetes.

In fact, many patients who already have diabetes have seen great results using a gastric sleeve to overcome this disease.

Besides a reduction in weight, there are other advantages to bariatric surgery, such as a decrease in appetite, which leads to greater self-control and greater metabolic rate.

Since this type of surgery requires hospitalization, it is expensive, and therefore, not everyone can afford it. In fact, many people cannot even access the procedure because many health plans do not offer them coverage for such surgeries.

The cost of bariatric surgery is one of the major barriers preventing people from getting the help they need.

This is why so many people have turned to gastric sleeve as an alternative.

By opting for this method, patients can get the benefits of bariatric surgery without the need for a traditional hospitalization.

The next step in its development would be 3D printed surgery, which would allow surgeons to eliminate the issues related to traditional surgery (such as infection or damage to internal organs) with minimal risk.

The gastric sleeve procedure was first developed in the 1940s and used during this time as a means for weight loss, but only as a temporary solution until other alternatives could be found.

It was introduced with wide attention after the release of the Atkins diet in 1972 by Dr. Robert Atkins.

Today, gastric sleeve is well known as a method of losing weight.

In fact, it is considered one of the simplest and most effective solutions for those who want to lose weight and even as an alternative to bariatric surgery.

It is used to treat not only overweight people but also those who are simply trying to get back in shape.

A person's body mass index (BMI) must be higher than 35 in order for him or her to qualify for this surgery. Patients with a BMI greater than 40 are generally considered obese, and those with a BMI greater than 45 should undergo gastric bypass surgery instead of a gastric sleeve.

In a gastric sleeve surgery, the stomach is reduced by turning part of it into a thin tube about 15 to 25 millimeters long.

The operation is minimally invasive and can be performed under local anesthesia.

It usually takes between 30 and 45 minutes to perform the procedure, which involves making a small incision in the abdomen and removing part of the stomach.

Once this has been done, another section of the stomach is connected to what remains.

The new gastric sleeve that forms acts as a restriction that limits food intake, thus helping patients lose weight.

The operation causes only temporary discomfort to patients, and most are able to leave the hospital 24 hours after surgery.

CHAPTER 1
Your New Bariatric Lifestyle & Your New Mindset Changing Your Habits & Creating Lifestyle Change

Steps and Strategies for Success

Before your surgery, there are some things you can do ahead of time that will help you during those painful days.

- **Change your diet**

You need to preparation timer your body for this direction by going on a high-protein liquid diet one or two weeks before your surgery. This will shrink your liver, making the surgery safer for you.

- **Change your grocery list**

You need to have a lot of protein-rich liquids before surgery and after surgery. Clear liquids are what you will consume immediately after your surgery for a day or two. After that phase, you will advance to protein shakes and pureed food.

- **Get the clothes you will need**

You will need transition clothes for the various weights that you will be. You will want your initial clothing after the surgery to fit loosely. You will also want slip-on shoes so that you won't have to bend over to tie your shoes.

- **Stop smoking**

Surgeons take smoking seriously. Just before surgery, they will likely give you a blood test to see whether you have been smoking lately. If you have, they will cancel your surgery. Why? If you are smoke-free, your recovery will be quicker. You will need to quit smoking one month before your surgery.

- **Pack your hospital bag**

You will stay at the hospital one night, so pack whatever you will need for one night.

- **Preparation timer your support group**

You will need both physical and mental support after your surgery. You need to educate people before your surgery and line up volunteers who can help you while you recover.

- **Get your insurance or another financing source ready**

Check if your insurance pays for this kind of surgery. Typically, body mass index and other health issues are involved. Get the financials ready to pay for your surgery.

- **Get ahead of the household chores and shopping before surgery**

Make lots of smoothies (minus the ice cubes), cook and freeze meals, clean the house and do all of the laundry before you go in for surgery so that nobody has to do those things later. Buy the stool softeners, over-the-counter medications and your prescriptions (if possible) ahead of time.

Your friends and family may help you, but it would be easier for everyone if you have most of the work done ahead of time. You will also be certain to not lack for anything while you are at a disadvantage.

- **Get the facts**

Talk to your surgeon about any concerns or questions you have about your surgery so that you have a good understanding about what will be done and be less anxious about your surgery.

- **Study up on proteins**

You will need to consume a lot of protein after your surgery. You need to try protein powders to discover which ones you like among the ones that won't add a lot of calories. Food sources are peanut butter, legumes, chicken, meats, and protein shakes.

After your surgery

- **Follow your doctor's prescribed diet**

Eat what your doctor tells you to eat after your surgery, which will consist of a lot of liquid. If you eat regular food too early or if you eat sugary or fat food, you may damage your stomach or harm yourself.

- **Skip work until you have healed**

Depending on which kind of surgery you have and what type of work you do, you could be back to work as soon as two weeks after surgery if you do not lift anything heavy.

- **Exercise when you can**

Wait about four weeks before you exercise or lift weights so that you will decrease the chance that you will get a hernia in the wound.

- **Go to your check-ups**

Let your doctor check on your progress at the scheduled times. He'll see whether or not you are on schedule in your weight loss goals.

- **Continue to find suitable foods you can eat**

You need to try out new recipes so that you can stay on your diet plan. You don't want boredom with your food to turn you back to your old eating habits.

- **Take multivitamins**

It will be hard to get all of the nutrition that you need from just your food, especially less food, so be sure to take a multivitamin daily.

- **Know when to ask for help**

Right after your surgery, it will be hard to get anything done. Hopefully, you got your chores done, groceries and meds purchased, food pre-made and frozen, and your helpers lined up before you went into surgery. Don't be afraid to call on the friends and family who agreed to help you when you need them, especially if you notice a complication.

- **Follow your prescription**

Keep taking your prescribed medication for as long as you were supposed to take it. Don't get off of it early. Make an appointment with your doctor if you have discomfort beyond what is normal.

- **Count the calories**

If you keep your calorie intake between 600 and 800 per day, you will lose weight. Consult your doctor for his suggested calorie target. Don't eat high-calorie food, especially those with sugar and/or fat.

- **Don't drink your calories**

Drink water, unsweetened ice tea, and sugar-free juice. You will need to use up your daily allotment of calories on food that contains protein instead of drinks with "empty calories."

CHAPTER 2
Post Operation Life

Post-op Gastric Bypass Surgery Diet

The moment the surgery is complete; your new diet begins in full force. The aim of the diet is to help you recover in the best way possible. The gastric bypass diet comes in various stages. Each stage shows that you are healing a little bit more. As you progress, you can go a little higher in your gastric bypass surgery diet. For easy remembering, the gastric bypass surgery has been divided into 5 stages. These stages do not include the pre-op diet. They are simply for the post-op diet.

Stage 1—Clear liquids

The first stage includes only liquids. This stage starts after the surgery. For about 1–7 days after the surgery, the patient can take only clear liquids. Your dietician will let you know exactly how long to stay in this stage.

Stage 2A—Full liquid

This diet includes full liquids. Full liquids are semi-liquid and are not see-through. It is midway between clear liquids and pureed foods. Here, your liquids can start to have some chunks of solid foods. This stage lasts for 1–2 weeks

Stage 2B—Pureed foods

After that stage, this next one lasts for 1–2 weeks. Here, you can consume liquid forms of protein. You should be taking up to 70 grams of protein and 64 ounces of fluids.

Stage 3—Soft foods

In this stage, patients can begin to eat soft foods that can be easily mashed. You should be taking up to 70 grams of protein and 64 ounces of clear water. You should also eat about 1–2 ounces in each serving. You should also take a very little portion of healthy fats. Usually, this comes from an avocado.

Stage 4—Solid foods

Here you can go back to eating solid foods. This diet starts from that point to the rest of your life. You should eat mainly protein and vegetables. The grains you consume should be in limited quantities. Your intake of sugar should be at the barest minimum. This will be your stage for the rest of your life.

Dos and don'ts of gastric bypass surgery diet

As expected, there are some things you are simply not allowed to do when it comes to your gastric bypass diet. Here are some of them.

1. No straw—This applies from stage 1 to stage 3. You should not use straws to take in your liquids. This is because using straws can take in unwanted air into the stomach.

2. Do not eat more than one new food per day—Your body will have different reactions to new foods even though you have eaten them before the surgery. Anything you haven't eaten after the surgery is a new food. Do not try more than one per day.

3. Learn how to chew—The way that you used to chew before the surgery is no longer the way you will chew. Before, chewing was a careless thing we did. However, now, you must learn how to chew again. Time yourself to ensure that you chew each bite for as long as 15-seconds.

4. Drink water—At stage four, drink at least 64 ounces of water each day. Take water 30 minutes after food.

5. Avoid processed carbs and sugar—Stay away from foods that have high levels of sugar and refined or processed carbohydrates.

6. Stay away from unhealthy fats—Make sure you avoid foods that have unhealthy fat.

7. Learn how to eat—Learn to chew proteins first. When they are eaten, eat your vegetables, and then carbohydrates.

Food Cravings After Gastric Surgery

After your gastric bypass surgery, you may find that you encounter a lot of cravings. It is only natural and you can be assured that after some time, your body will adjust and you will have few cravings. In case you have cravings, here are some tips to help you manage them.

1. Invest in healthy snacks—Purchase healthy snacks. When you purchase healthy snacks, you can have them when you are hungry to take your mind off food cravings.

2. Do not skip meals—To succeed in this diet, you must find balance. Finding your balance involves eating when you should and when you shouldn't. Skipping one meal can put in discord to your hard work as your stomach is now extremely sensitive.

3. Drink water—In a day, ensure you have as many as 8 glasses. When you are craving, take a big gulp or two.

4. Plan your environments—Do not go to a fast-food restaurant where everyone will be eating what you can't eat. Plan your environments. Plan where you are supposed to stay.

5. Distract yourself—Distracting yourself when you are cravings will help you out. Get up and do something you like.

CHAPTER 3
Tips for After Surgery

You'll also want to read up on some tips for handing things after the surgery as well. For example, your entire lifestyle ahead will be in for a lot of change. You won't be allowed to eat anything for several days to allow your stomach to heal up, and your diet in the recovery period will be drastically different. How often you make it to the medical clinic will also increase so your health can be monitored and you can have your blood tested.

Your entire body and even your mental state (hopefully temporarily!) will be different than it was before. As you begin to lose weight at a rapid weight, you'll feel things such as body aches, fatigue, feeling cold, thinning hair, and dry skin. How you handle these changes in your life will be just as important as how you handle preparations before the gastric sleeve surgery as well.

Here are some tips for after gastric sleeve surgery:

Listen to Your Doctor!

You don't want to go through the entire surgical procedure only to not lose as much weight as you expected you would. Following the specific instructions set to you by your doctor will be the most important thing you can do to ensuring the aftermath of the gastric sleeve surgery is successful. Besides, don't avoid any check-ups with your doctor as well. While medical check-ups may be time-consuming, they are important to keeping you on the right track.

Only Work When You Are Ready

If you feel physically uncomfortable about returning to work during the recovery time, that's perfectly fine. In fact, the average patient of gastric sleeve surgery takes up to two weeks before they are fully healed enough to head back to work. Don't feel ashamed if you don't feel you are ready yet.

Get Plenty of Exercises

It will take time to get into the habit of exercise and to exercise successfully, but doing so will allow your body to strengthen and dealing with the loss of calorie intake. You can start some simple exercise programs, such as walking, swimming.

Learn More

Don't hesitate to continue to learn as much more as you can after the surgery. You can look into what new recipes you can try or what some different exercising tips that exist out there.

Receive Plenty of Support

Any patient who goes through gastric sleeve surgery will need the support of family and friends following the surgery. Don't feel nervous about asking for help. In fact, most of the people you are close with will probably be glad to help you along on your journey.

Take Your Medications

Don't try to phase out of taking your medication. If you have any discomfort with your existing medication, speak with your doctor or a member of the medical staff before quitting taking them. If you don't follow your medical prescription, the surgery may not be as successful as it should be. In addition to your medications, take plenty of multivitamins. Multivitamins should be prescribed to you anyway, but if they aren't, know that multivitamins are necessary for your body to get the nutrition it loses from the decrease in food intake.

Calories

Calories, calories, calories. Obviously, by consuming less food, your body will be in taking fewer calories. However, you also want to keep yourself at 600 to 800 calories per day; otherwise, the aftermath of the surgery may not be a success. If the specific number of calories you need to intake is different from the typical six hundred to eight hundred range, your doctor will let you know. Keep track of your daily caloric intake and educate yourself on how many calories are in the foods and liquids you consume. If you can adhere to a daily regimen, you'll keep your calorie intake right where it needs to be.

Avoid Alcohol

Finally, you'll want to avoid drinking alcohol after surgery. Doing so can have drastic effects on your recovery time and your weight loss in general.

CHAPTER 4
Meal Plan Challenge

Planning Your Meals

Have an idea of what you plan to eat throughout the week will save you lots of time and money, and it will also minimize the choices you need to make around meals. Now, I don't want you to be overwhelmed with the idea of meal planning. It doesn't have to be time-consuming or difficult, and your plan certainly does not need to be followed. Start simple, and think of a few ideas of what you might like to have for breakfasts, lunches, dinners, and snacks in between. Make sure you have the ingredients you'll need on hand, and then you'll have options when it comes time to eat.

Meal-planning Tips

Choose recipes with the same ingredients to reduce food waste and save money.

Choose a shopping day, and make a shopping list before you go. Keep breakfasts and snacks simple. Cook once; eat twice. Freeze leftovers for easy meals throughout the week.

The 10-week Meal Plan

Your surgeon's recommendations may differ from this transitional plan, so be sure to consult with your doctor before advancing between phases.

As part of the plan, you will find ideas for how to incorporate physical activity into your life. These exercises are tailored to each stage of your recovery.

Adaptations for Band and Sleeve Patients

Gastric band, sleeve, and bypass directions vary widely in surgical complexity, which will dictate the length of recovery and transition back to regular textures in your diet. Always consult with your care team before making any dietary changes, but here are some guidelines for adjusting the meal plan to your specific needs.

Adjustable Gastric Band

Most gastric band patients will progress to soft foods after 4 weeks and a general diet after 5 or 6 weeks. However, roughly 6 weeks after your band placement, you may receive your first saline fill. After your band is placed, and following each subsequent fill, you will need to adhere to a transitional diet, from full liquids back to solids as tolerated, usually over a span of 7 to 10 days.

Laparoscopic Sleeve Gastrectomy

Due to the complexity of the gastric sleeve surgeries, the length of transitional diet and recovery periods are different from patient to patient. Typically, sleeve patients follow a full-liquid diet for 2 weeks, a purée diet for another week, and a soft-foods diet for 3 weeks before returning to normal textures as tolerated 6 weeks post-op.

The First 8 Weeks

A transitional diet in the first 8 weeks after surgery is essential for proper healing. Be sure to stay mindful while you eat, as you may not have a true understanding of the capacity of your new pouch. If you have any difficulty after advancing your diet to the next phase, return to the previous stage for a few days.

Liquids

After surgery, you'll begin with a full-liquid diet. Liquid textures require minimal work for your stomach to digest, allowing it to heal appropriately. Your primary goal during this stage is to stay hydrated, but you will also be using protein drinks to reach your protein targets necessary for recovery.

Puréed foods

After 1 to 2 weeks of tolerating liquids, you can begin transitioning to a purée diet. Foods at this stage should have the consistency of a smooth paste—no solid pieces or chunks. Foods that purée well include soft meats with sauce, fruits, cooked vegetables, low-fat dairy items, eggs, low-fiber hot cereals, legumes, and low-fat soups. Most can be puréed in a good blender or food processor.

Because of stomach capacity restrictions, you will want to limit your portions to about 2 to 3 ounces (4 to 8 tablespoons) at a time. Consider adding unflavored protein powder or fat-free powdered milk to your foods, or continue using protein shakes to reach your protein goal (at least 60 grams per day).

As you transition from liquids to purées, it is important you stay hydrated, drinking 48 ounces of fluids per day, including protein shakes. Also, remember that you shouldn't drink with meals; wait at least 30 min after you finish eating.

Now that your body's healing, you can begin low-impact exercises to build strength and flexibility. You can also begin taking longer walks or walking more quickly.

Helpful tips

- If you experience changes in taste, like sensitivity to sweetness, consider adding spices or dried herbs to food and shakes.
- If you have nausea or discomfort while eating, take smaller bites, and make sure you eat very slowly.
- If you do not have much of an appetite, continue using protein shakes to meet your daily goals.
- If you are having difficulty tolerating meats, try something softer, with more moisture.
- If you are having difficulty drinking enough fluids (48 to 64 ounces per day), use protein shakes to reach your protein goal and stay hydrated. If you are not feeling hungry, set alarms to remind yourself to eat.
- Try only 1 or 2 new foods at a time.

Soft Foods

A soft-foods diet offers more texture for your tastes, but you still need to be able to cut through your food with a fork. Food pieces should be small, tender, and easy to chew. As you transition to a soft-foods diet, make sure you try only one or two new foods at a time. Some possibilities for this stage include ground lean meat or poultry, flaky fish, eggs, cottage cheese, yogurt, soft cheese, hot cereal, canned or soft fresh fruits (without seeds or skin), cooked vegetables (without skin), beans, and lentils.

You will likely be eating at least 3 meals with 1 to 2 protein-rich snacks or shakes to meet your goal of 60 to 80 grams of protein per day. Each meal should consist of 1/3 to ½ cup of food. Continue to avoid drinking while you eat. Wait 30 min after a meal to hydrate.

CHAPTER 5
Soups

1. Bean Tomato Broth

PREPARATION TIME
15'

COOK TIME
1h 20'

SERVING
6

INGREDIENTS

- 2 lbs. medium-sized tomatoes, pureed
- 1 cup kidney beans, pre-cooked
- 1 small onion, diced
- 2 garlic cloves, crushed
- 1 cup heavy cream
- 1 cup vegetable broth
- 2 tbsp. fresh parsley, finely chopped
- ¼ tsp black pepper, ground
- 2 tbsp. extra-virgin olive oil
- 1 tsp dry oregano, ground
- ½ tsp salt
- ¼ tsp chili pepper, ground

DIRECTIONS

1. Soak the beans overnight. Rinse and drain well and place the beans in a deep pot. Add 4 cups of water and bring it to a boil. Cook for 30 minutes and then remove from the heat. Drain and set aside.
2. Wash the tomatoes and cut them into bite-sized pieces. Transfer to a food processor and add some salt and oregano. Blend until smooth and creamy and set aside.
3. Now, preheat the oil in a large saucepan over medium-high temperature. Add onions and garlic and stir-fry for 5 minutes, or until translucent. Add beans, tomatoes, and broth. Stir well and bring it to a boil. Reduce the heat to low and sprinkle with chili. Stir well and cook for 35–40 minutes. Add heavy cream and cook for 2 more minutes, stirring constantly.
4. Remove from the heat and set aside to cool for a while. Now, drain the liquid into a serving bowl. Sprinkle with some finely chopped parsley and enjoy!

NUTRITION

Calories: 254
Protein: 9.7g
Total Carbs: 27.1g

Dietary Fibers: 6.9g
Total Fat: 13g

2. Spinach Veal Broth

PREPARATION TIME
15'

COOK TIME
1h 10'

SERVING
4

INGREDIENTS

- 1 lb. veal steak, cut into bite-sized pieces
- 1 lb. fresh spinach, torn
- 3 large eggs, beaten
- 4 cups vegetable broth
- 1 small onion, finely chopped
- 2 garlic cloves
- 3 tbsp. extra-virgin olive oil
- 1 tsp salt

DIRECTIONS

1. Wash the meat under cold running water and pat dry with kitchen paper. Cut into bite-sized pieces and place in a medium bowl. Generously sprinkle with salt and pepper and stir well with your hands. Set aside.
2. Rinse spinach thoroughly and drain. Cut into bite-sized pieces and set aside.
3. Preheat the oil in a large skillet over medium-high temperature. Add meat and cook for 5 minutes, stirring occasionally. Add garlic and onions and give it a good stir. Cook for another 3–4 minutes, or until the onions are translucent.
4. Now, add vegetable broth and spinach. Bring it to a boil and then whisk in the eggs. Reduce the heat to low and cook for about an hour. Remove from the heat. Using a large sieve, remove the meat and vegetables from the liquid.
5. Add some salt if needed and pour the broth into a serving glass.
6. Enjoy!

NUTRITION

Calories: 416
Protein: 43g
Total Carbs: 7.5g

Dietary Fibers: 2.9g
Total Fat: 23.9g

3. Carrot Lentil Broth

PREPARATION TIME
10'

COOK TIME
25'

SERVING
3

INGREDIENTS

- 1 cup red lentils, soaked overnight
- 4 large carrots, peeled and chopped
- 1 medium-sized onion, peeled and finely chopped
- 3 tbsp. milk
- 1 tbsp. all-purpose flour
- ½ tsp black pepper, freshly ground
- ½ tsp cumin, ground
- ½ tsp salt
- 2 tbsp. olive oil

DIRECTIONS

1. Wash and peel the carrots. Place them in a food processor and add milk. Blend until smooth and creamy. Set aside.
2. After soaking the lentils overnight, rinse well and drain. Place in a deep pot of boiling water and cook for 15 minutes. Remove from the heat and drain. Set aside.
3. Preheat the oil in a large saucepan over a medium-high temperature. Add onions and flour. Stir-fry for 5 minutes, or until translucent.
4. Now, add carrot puree and lentils. Sprinkle with salt and pepper to taste and stir well. Cook for 1 minute and then add 4 cups of water. Stir well and bring it to a boil. Reduce the heat to low and cook for 1 hour. Remove from the heat.
5. Drain the liquid into a separate bowl and serve immediately.

NUTRITION

Calories: 228,
Protein: 11.1g
Total Carbs: 32.7g

Dietary Fibers: 13.7g
Total Fat: 6.3g

4. Celery Spinach Broth

PREPARATION TIME
15'

COOK TIME
45'

SERVING
6

INGREDIENTS

- 1 lb. fresh celery, chopped
- 1 lb. fresh spinach, chopped
- 1 medium-sized red onion, finely chopped
- 1 cup heavy cream
- 1 cup water
- 1 cup sour cream
- 2 cups vegetable broth
- 2 tbsp. butter

- ½ tsp dried thyme, ground
- ½ tsp salt
- ½ tsp black pepper, ground

DIRECTIONS

1. Combine celery and spinach in a large colander. Wash thoroughly under cold running water. Drain and chop into small pieces. Set aside.
2. Melt the butter in a large saucepan over medium-high temperature. Add onions and stir-fry until translucent. Add celery and spinach. Sprinkle with salt, thyme and pepper. Stir well and cook for about 3–4 minutes, or until celery and spinach are tender.
3. Add the vegetable broth and water. Stir well and bring it to a boil. Reduce the heat to low and cover with a lid. Cook for 15–20 minutes and then stir in the heavy cream and sour cream. Cook for another 5 minutes and remove from the heat.
4. Cover with a lid and cook for 20 minutes. Remove from the heat and stir in the heavy cream. Using a large sieve, separate the vegetables from the broth. Let it cool for a while and store in a glass jar.
5. Refrigerate up to 2 days or serve immediately.

NUTRITION

Calories: 235
Protein: 6.2g
Total Carbs: 9.4g

Dietary Fibers: 3.3g
Total Fat: 20.2g

5. Carrot Coconut Broth

PREPARATION TIME
15'

COOK TIME
20'

SERVING
6

INGREDIENTS

- 6 large carrots, thinly sliced
- 2 cups coconut milk
- 1 medium-sized sweet potato, chopped
- 1 small onion, chopped
- 2 cups chicken broth
- 1 tsp curry powder
- 2 garlic cloves, crushed
- 1 tbsp. vegetable oil
- 1 tsp salt
- ¼ tsp black pepper, ground

DIRECTIONS

1. Preheat the oil in a deep pot over a medium-high temperature. Add onions and stir-fry them until translucent. Add garlic and mix well with onions. Cook for another minute.
2. Add carrots, potatoes, and chicken broth. Bring it to a boil and sprinkle with curry, salt, and pepper. Cook for 15 minutes and then add coconut milk. Cook until heated through and remove from the heat.
3. Now, separate the broth and vegetables. Store the broth in a glass jar and refrigerate for up to 2 days.

NUTRITION

Calories: 271
Protein: 4.7g
Total Carbs: 17.4g

Dietary Fibers: 4.6g
Total Fat: 21.9g

6. Eggplant Tomato Soup

PREPARATION TIME
10'

COOK TIME
20'

SERVING
4

INGREDIENTS

- 2 medium-sized eggplants, peeled and cubed
- 2 large tomatoes, peeled and diced
- 1 medium-sized red onion, finely chopped
- 2 tbsp. olive oil
- 1 tsp salt
- ½ tsp black pepper, ground
- ½ cup sour cream
- ½ tsp dried oregano, ground

DIRECTIONS

1. Peel the eggplants and cut them into small cubes. Set aside.
2. Wash and peel the tomatoes. Chop into small pieces and set aside.
3. Preheat the oil in a large skillet over medium-high temperature. Add onions and stir-fry for 3 minutes, and then add eggplants. Stir well and cook for 5 minutes. Add diced tomatoes and stir well. Pour 1 cup of water and bring it to a boil, stirring occasionally.
4. Remove from the heat and set aside to cool. Transfer to a food processor in batches. Blend until nicely pureed.
5. Return to the pot and add about 3 cups of water. Bring it to a boil and then stir in the sour cream and oregano. Cook until heated through and remove from the heat.
6. Serve warm.

NUTRITION

Calories: 207
Protein: 4.3g
Total Carbs: 21.1g

Dietary Fibers: 9.9g
Total Fat: 13.7g

7. Sage Soup

PREPARATION TIME
5'

COOK TIME
30'

SERVING
4

INGREDIENTS

- 2 cups fresh sage, roughly chopped
- 1 medium-sized onion, finely chopped
- 1 tbsp. all-purpose flour
- 1 cup bone broth
- 1 tsp cayenne pepper, ground
- ½ tsp garlic powder
- 2 tbsp. olive oil
- ½ cup sour cream

DIRECTIONS

1. Wash the sage thoroughly under cold running water. Drain well and place in a deep pot. Add enough water to cover and bring it to a boil. Cook for 1 minute and remove from the heat and drain well. Set aside.
2. Preheat the oil in a large skillet over medium-high temperature. Add onion and stir-fry for 3 minutes, or until translucent. Add flour, garlic, and ½ cup of water. Reduce the heat to low and simmer for 2 more minutes. Add broth and 1 cup of water. Bring it to a boil and then add sage. Cook for 15 minutes and then remove from the heat. Let it cool for a while.
3. Transfer all to a food processor and pulse until creamy. Return to the pot and stir in the sour cream.
4. Serve immediately.

NUTRITION

Calories: 214
Protein: 8.2g
Total Carbs: 15.5g

Dietary Fibers: 7.2g
Total Fat: 15.2g

8. Acorn Squash Cream Soup

PREPARATION TIME
15'

COOK TIME
1h 5'

SERVING
6

INGREDIENTS

- 2 medium-sized acorn squash
- 4 cups chicken broth
- 3 garlic cloves, finely chopped
- 3 tbsp. olive oil
- 2 tbsp. lime juice, freshly squeezed
- 1 medium-sized onion, roughly chopped
- ½ cup sour cream
- 1 tsp black pepper, ground
- ½ tsp salt

DIRECTIONS

1. Preheat the oven to 350°F.
2. Cut the squash lengthwise in half and scoop out the seeds. Place it on a large baking sheet and set it aside.
3. Peel the onion and cut it into large pieces. Spread evenly over the squash.
4. In a small bowl, combine olive oil and garlic. Drizzle over the squash. Place it in the oven and bake for about 40–45 minutes, or until nicely tender. Remove from the oven and allow it to cool completely.
5. Now, transfer all to a large saucepan and add the remaining ingredients.
6. Cover with a lid and cook for 15 minutes at low temperature. Transfer to a food processor and blend until smooth and creamy.
7. Stir in the sour cream and reheat. Sprinkle with some more salt and pepper if you like. However, it's optional.
8. Serve warm.

NUTRITION

Calories: 195
Protein: 5.3g
Total Carbs: 18.8g

Dietary Fibers: 2.7g
Total Fat: 12.1g

9. Creamy Leek Soup

PREPARATION TIME
15'

COOK TIME
20'

SERVING
3

INGREDIENTS

- 1 cup leeks, chopped
- 1 medium-sized potato
- 1 large carrot, chopped
- 1 cup chicken stock, unsalted
- 1 cup milk, low-fat
- 1 cup spinach, finely chopped
- 1 tbsp. parsley, finely chopped
- ¼ tsp black pepper, ground

DIRECTIONS

1. Wash and prepare the vegetables. Place the leeks, spinach, and celery in a pot of boiling water. Cook for 3 minutes and remove from the heat. Drain well and set aside.
2. Place the potato in a pot of boiling water and cook for 5 minutes, or until slightly tender. Remove from the heat and drain well. Set aside.
3. Now, combine leeks, potato, carrot, and spinach in a heavy-bottomed pot. Pour the chicken stock and milk. Sprinkle with pepper and parsley. Bring it to a boil and then reduce the heat to low. Simmer for 15 minutes and remove from the heat. Transfer all to a food processor and pulse until creamy and pureed. Return to the pot and reheat.
4. Serve warm.

NUTRITION

Calories: 130
Protein: 5.3g
Total Carbs: 23.8g

Dietary Fibers: 3g
Total Fat: 2.1g

10. Green Cream Soup

PREPARATION TIME
5'

COOK TIME
15'

SERVING
2

INGREDIENTS

- 1 cup fresh broccoli, chopped
- 1 cup cauliflower, chopped
- 4 tbsp. fresh parsley, finely chopped
- ¼ tsp chili pepper, ground
- 1 tsp dried thyme, ground
- ½ cup milk, low-fat

DIRECTIONS

1. Place broccoli and cauliflower in a heavy-bottomed pot. Add enough water to cover all ingredients and bring it to a boil. Cook for 5 minutes, or until tender. Remove from the heat and drain well. Set aside to cool for a while.
2. Transfer cooked broccoli and cauliflower to a blender. Add ½ cup of water and sprinkle with chili pepper. Process until pureed and transfer to a clean heavy-bottomed pot.
3. Add 2 cups of water and sprinkle with finely chopped parsley. Bring to a boil and reduce the heat to low. Cook for 2 minutes. Add milk and give it a good stir. Cook for five more minutes over medium-high heat.
4. Serve warm.

NUTRITION

Calories: 63
Protein: 4.6g
Total Carbs: 9.5g

Dietary Fibers: 2.9g
Total Fat: 1.6g

11. Spinach Potato Cream Soup

PREPARATION TIME
15'

COOK TIME
35'

SERVING
6

INGREDIENTS

- 1 lb. fresh spinach, chopped
- 2 medium-sized potatoes, chopped
- 3 tbsp. fresh parsley, chopped
- 1 small onion, finely chopped
- 2 tbsp. olive oil
- 2 tbsp. all-purpose flour

- 2 cups chicken broth
- 1 cup cream cheese
- ½ tsp cayenne pepper
- 1 tsp salt
- ¼ tsp black pepper, ground

DIRECTIONS

1. Rinse the spinach thoroughly under cold running water. Drain well and chop into small pieces. Set aside.
2. Peel the potatoes and chop them into bite-sized pieces. Set aside.
3. Place the spinach in a pot of boiling water and cook for 3 minutes, or until tender. Remove from the heat and drain. Set aside.
4. Place the potatoes in a pot of boiling water and sprinkle them with some salt. Bring it to a boil and cook for 10 minutes. Remove from the heat and drain. Set aside.
5. Preheat the oil in a large skillet over a medium-high temperature. Add onion and stir-fry until translucent. Stir in the flour, cayenne pepper, and 1 tablespoon of water. Cook for 1 minute, stirring constantly. Remove from the heat.
6. In a large heavy-bottomed pot, pour chicken broth and 1 cup of water. Bring it to a boil over a medium-high temperature.
7. Add spinach and potatoes and sprinkle with pepper. Cook for 10 minutes, and reduce heat to low. Cook for another 5 minutes and then stir in the sour cream and parsley.
8. Now, transfer all to a food processor in few batches. Pulse until creamy and pureed. Transfer to the pot and stir in the flour mixture. Cook for 2 more minutes.
9. Remove from the heat and set aside to cool for a while before serving.

NUTRITION

Calories: 270
Protein: 8.4g
Total Carbs: 18.6g

Dietary Fibers: 3.8g
Total Fat: 19.1g

12. Chicken Cauliflower Soup

PREPARATION TIME
10'

COOK TIME
25'

SERVING
4

INGREDIENTS

- 10 oz. chicken fillets, cut into bite-sized pieces
- 1 cup cauliflower, chopped
- 1 tsp fresh mint, finely chopped
- ¼ tsp dry coriander, crushed
- 1 tbsp. olive oil
- ½ tsp salt
- ¼ tsp black pepper

DIRECTIONS

1. Wash the cauliflower thoroughly and remove the outer leaves. Cut into small pieces and fill the measuring cup. Reserve the rest in the refrigerator.
2. Place the cauliflower and dry coriander into a deep pot. Add enough water to cover and bring it to a boil. Cook for about 10–15 minutes. Remove from the heat and blend the soup with a stick blender. Set aside.
3. Now, preheat the oil in a large skillet over a medium-high temperature. Add meat chops and sprinkle with some salt and pepper. Cook for 5–8 minutes, or until golden brown. Remove from the heat and add it to the soup.
4. Now, transfer all to a food processor. Pulse until creamy and well combined. Return the soup to the pot and reheat.
5. Garnish with fresh mint before serving and enjoy!

NUTRITION

Calories: 171
Protein: 21g
Total Carbs: 1.5g

Dietary Fibers: 0.7g
Total Fat: 8.8g

13. Zucchini Cream Soup

PREPARATION TIME
10'

COOK TIME
40'

SERVING
3

INGREDIENTS

- 1 lb. zucchini, chopped
- 3 cups vegetable broth
- 1 small onion, chopped
- 2 cups milk, low-fat
- 4 tbsp. Greek yogurt
- 1 tsp fresh sage, finely chopped
- 1 garlic clove, crushed
- 1 tsp olive oil
- ½ tsp salt
- ¼ tsp black pepper, ground

DIRECTIONS

1. Peel the zucchinis and chop them into bite-sized pieces. Set aside.
2. Peel the onion and chop it into small pieces. Set aside.
3. Preheat the oil in a heavy-bottomed pot over medium-high temperature. Add onion and garlic and stir-fry until translucent.
4. Now, add the zucchini chops and sprinkle with some sage to taste. Pour the vegetable broth and stir all well. Bring it to a boil and then reduce the heat to low. Cover with a lid and cook for about 25–30 minutes more. Remove from the heat and set aside to cool for a while.
5. Transfer all to the food processor and blend until creamy. Now, return to the pot and heat up. Sprinkle with salt and pepper and remove from the heat.
6. Stir in the Greek yogurt and milk.
7. Serve warm.

NUTRITION

Calories: 162
Protein: 15.5g
Total Carbs: 13.3g

Dietary Fibers: 1.4g
Total Fat: 5.6g

14. Broccoli Gorgonzola Soup

PREPARATION TIME
10'

COOK TIME
2 hours

SERVING
6

INGREDIENTS

- 10 oz. Gorgonzola cheese, crumbled
- 1 cup broccoli, finely chopped
- 1 tbsp. olive oil
- ½ cup full-fat milk
- ½ cup vegetable broth
- 1 tbsp. parsley, finely chopped
- ½ tsp salt
- ¼ tsp black pepper, ground

DIRECTIONS

1. Wash the broccoli under cold running water. Drain and chop into bite-sized pieces. Set aside.
2. Grease the bottom of a deep pot with olive oil. Add all ingredients and three cups of water. Mix well with a kitchen whisker until fully combined.
3. Cover with a lid and cook for 2 hours at low temperature.
4. Remove from the heat and sprinkle with some fresh parsley for extra taste.
5. I like to stir in one tablespoon of Greek yogurt before serving, but it's optional.

NUTRITION

Calories: 204
Protein: 11.9g
Total Carbs: 5.1g

Dietary Fibers: 1.9g
Total Fat: 16.5g

15. Chickpea Pepper Soup

PREPARATION TIME
5'

COOK TIME
40'

SERVING
4

INGREDIENTS

- 14 oz. chickpeas, soaked
- 2 large red bell peppers, finely chopped
- 2 small onions, peeled and finely chopped
- 2 large tomatoes, peeled and finely chopped
- 3 tbsp. tomato paste
- Handful fresh parsley, finely chopped
- 2 cups vegetable broth
- 3 tbsp. extra virgin olive oil
- 1 tsp salt

DIRECTIONS

1. Soak the chickpeas overnight. Rinse and drain. Place the chickpeas in a pot of boiling water and cook for 30 minutes. Remove from the heat and drain. Set aside.
2. Wash the bell pepper and cut lengthwise in half. Remove the seeds and finely chop them. Set aside.
3. Preheat the oil in a large saucepan over medium-high temperature. Add onions and bell peppers. Cook for 5 minutes, or until tender. Add tomatoes, tomato paste, and parsley. Stir well and cook for 2 minutes. Now, add chickpeas and broth. Sprinkle with salt and stir again. Bring it to a boil and reduce the heat to low. Cook for 30 minutes and remove from the heat.
4. Serve warm.

NUTRITION

Calories: 353
Protein: 15.9g
Total Carbs: 49.5g

Dietary Fibers: 13.6g
Total Fat: 11.7g

16. Fresh Tomato and Celery Soup

PREPARATION TIME
10'

COOK TIME
30'

SERVING
4

INGREDIENTS

- 1 lb. tomatoes, peeled and roughly chopped
- 3.5 oz. celery root, finely chopped
- ¼ cup fresh celery leaves, finely chopped
- 1 tbsp. fresh basil, finely chopped
- Salt and pepper to taste
- 5 tbsp. extra virgin olive oil

DIRECTIONS

1. Preheat the oil in a large non-stick frying pan over a medium-high temperature. Add finely chopped celery root, celery leaves, and fresh basil. Season with salt and pepper and stir-fry for about 10 minutes, until nicely browned.
2. Add chopped tomatoes and about ¼ cup of water. Reduce the heat to the minimum and cook for 15 minutes, stirring constantly, until softened. Now add about 4 cups of water (or vegetable broth) and bring it to a boil. Give it a good stir and remove from the heat.
3. Top with fresh parsley and serve.

NUTRITION

Calories: 122
Protein: 1.4g
Total Carbs: 6.9g

Dietary Fibers: 1.9g
Total Fats: 10.8g

17. Creamy Wild Asparagus Soup

PREPARATION TIME
10'

COOK TIME
20'

SERVING
6

INGREDIENTS

- 2 lbs. fresh wild asparagus, trimmed
- 2 small onions, peeled and finely chopped
- 1 cup heavy cream
- 4 cups of vegetable broth
- 2 tbsp. butter
- 1 tbsp. vegetable oil
- ½ tsp salt
- ½ tsp dried oregano
- ½ tsp cayenne pepper

DIRECTIONS

1. Rinse and drain asparagus. Cut into about one-inch thick pieces. Set aside.
2. Melt the butter in a large skillet and add oil. Heat up and add onions. Cook until translucent.
3. Now add trimmed asparagus, oregano, salt, and cayenne pepper. Stir well and continue to cook until asparagus soften.
4. Add the vegetable broth and mix well to combine. Cook for 15 minutes, stirring occasionally.
5. Whisk in one cup of heavy cream and serve.

NUTRITION

Calories: 189
Protein: 7.3g
Total Carbs: 9.4g

Dietary Fibers: 3.8g
Total Fats: 14.7g

18. Homemade Chicken Soup

PREPARATION TIME
20'

COOK TIME
40'

SERVING
4

INGREDIENTS

- 1 lb. chicken meat
- ½ cup soup noodles
- 4 cups chicken broth
- A handful fresh parsley
- 1 tsp salt
- ¼ tsp freshly ground black pepper

DIRECTIONS

1. For this recipe, I always try to find an organic chicken. They are much tastier and better for homemade soup. Use both dark and white pieces and rinse well under the running water. Pat dry with kitchen paper and place on a clean work surface.
2. Using a sharp paring knife, cut chicken into bite-sized pieces. Sprinkle with salt and place in a deep pot. If using organic chicken, be careful not to add extra fat because this meat already has enough fat.
3. Pour in the chicken broth and cover with a lid. Cook for 45 minutes, over medium-high heat.
4. Now add soup noodles and reduce the heat to minimum. Cook for five more minutes.
5. Sprinkle with some freshly ground black pepper and parsley.
6. Serve warm.

NUTRITION

Calories: 267
Protein: 38.5g,
Total Carbs: 2.8g,

Dietary Fibers: 0.6g,
Total Fats: 10.2g

19. Butternut Squash Soup Broth

PREPARATION TIME
10'

COOK TIME
40'

SERVING
4-6

INGREDIENTS

- 2 tablespoons olive oil
- 2/3 cup onions, finely chopped
- 1 cup carrots, thinly sliced
- 1 large potato, peeled, cubed
- 2 cups butternut squash, peeled, cubed
- 1 Granny Smith apple, peeled, cored, cubed
- 4 cups chicken broth
- ¼ teaspoon nutmeg
- salt and pepper to taste
- ½ cup milk (optional)

DIRECTIONS

1. In a medium saucepan, heat olive oil; add onions and cook over low heat until softened, about 5 minutes.
2. Add carrots, potato, squash, apple, and chicken broth; cover and cook over low heat until vegetables are tender for about 30 minutes. Stir in nutmeg, salt and pepper.
3. Place half the mixture into a blender; blend until smooth. Pour into another saucepan or large bowl and blend the remaining half of the vegetables until smooth.
4. Return to saucepan; stir in milk if desired. Serve.

NUTRITION

Calories: 100
Total Fat: 2.5g
Total Carbohydrate: 20g

Protein: 2g

20. Simple Meatball Soup

PREPARATION TIME
10'

COOK TIME
1 hour

SERVING
4-6

INGREDIENTS

- 2 teaspoons olive oil
- 1 small onion, finely chopped
- 2 cloves garlic, finely chopped
- 2 cups tomato juice
- 2 cups chicken broth
- ½ cup water
- ¾ cup vegetable juice blend (such as V8)
- ½ cup green pepper, finely chopped
- 1/3 cup white quinoa, uncooked
- 24 meatballs, prepackaged, frozen

DIRECTIONS

1. In a large saucepan, heat olive oil; add garlic and onion, and allow to cook on medium heat until soft, about 5 mins.
2. Add tomato juice, broth, water, vegetable juice, and green pepper; bring to near boiling then reduce heat. Cover; cook over low heat for 30 minutes, or until onions and peppers are soft and flavors are well blended; stir occasionally.
3. Add quinoa and meatballs; cover and continue cooking for 25 minutes, or until quinoa is tender and meatballs are heated throughout.

NUTRITION

Calories: 277
Total Fat: 14g
Total Carbohydrate: 26 g

Protein: 13g

21. Chicken Barley Soup

PREPARATION TIME
10'

COOK TIME
1 hour

SERVING
6-8

INGREDIENTS

- 1-pound ground chicken
- 2 (14-ounce) cans of chicken broth
- 1 cup vegetable juice blend (such as V8)
- 4 cups water
- 1 cup carrots, peeled and thinly sliced
- ½ cup cabbage, finely shredded
- ½ cup green pepper, diced
- 1 cup onion, finely chopped
- 2 cloves garlic, minced
- 2 teaspoons seasoned salt
- ¾ cup barley, uncooked

DIRECTIONS

1. In a large saucepan, cook ground chicken, stirring until ground chicken is browned and crumbly. Drain fat
2. Add broth, juice, water, carrots, cabbage, green pepper, onion, garlic, seasoned salt and barley; stir.
3. Cover; cook over low heat for 1½-2 hours, or until barley is tender; stir occasionally.

NUTRITION

Calories: 90
Total Fat: 3g
Total Carbohydrate: 11 g

Protein: 5g

22. Ham and Bean Soup

PREPARATION TIME
10'

COOK TIME
5 hours

SERVING
8

INGREDIENTS

- ½ (16-ounce) package navy beans
- 14-ounce cans chicken broth
- 2 cups water
- 1 cup carrots, thinly sliced
- 1 cup onion, finely chopped
- 2 cloves garlic, sliced
- 1 (14-ounce) can diced tomatoes, with juice
- ½ teaspoon black pepper
- 1½ teaspoons seasoned salt
- 1 cup green cabbage, finely chopped
- 1 (5-ounce) can smoked ground ham

DIRECTIONS

1. Wash navy beans according to package directions.
2. In a large saucepan, heat 1-quart water to boiling. Remove from heat; add beans, cover and let sit for one hour to soften; drain.
3. Add broth, water, carrots, onion, garlic, tomatoes, pepper, seasoned salt, cabbage, and ham. Cover; cook on low heat for 3–4 hours, or until beans become very soft. Stir occasionally.
4. Using a potato masher, mash beans until about half of them are broken apart; stir to blend.

NUTRITION

Calories: 177
Total Fat: 2g
Total Carbohydrate: 26g

Protein: 14g

23. French Onion Soup

PREPARATION TIME
10'

COOK TIME
40'

SERVING
6

INGREDIENTS

- 1 tablespoon olive oil
- 2 cups sweet onions, finely chopped
- 4 cups chicken broth
- ½ cup dry red wine
- 1 teaspoon garlic, finely chopped
- 6 slices French bread, 1-inch thick
- 6 tablespoons Parmesan cheese, freshly grated

DIRECTIONS

1. In a large saucepan, add olive oil and onions; cook over medium heat, stirring often, until onions are browned.
2. Add broth, wine, and garlic; cover and cook over low heat for 25 minutes.
3. Meanwhile, toast bread until lightly browned; place one piece of toast in the bottom of individual soup bowls; sprinkle each toast with 1 tablespoon Parmesan cheese.
4. Pour soup over toast to serve.

NUTRITION

Calories: 190
Total Fat: 9g
Total Carbohydrate: 21g

Protein: 7g

24. Cheesy Cauliflower Soup

PREPARATION TIME
10'

COOK TIME
45'

SERVING
6-8

INGREDIENTS

- 3 tablespoons olive oil
- 3/4 cup onions, finely chopped
- 5 cups chicken broth
- 1 cup water
- 1 medium cauliflower, cut into florets
- 1/3 teaspoon rosemary
- 1/8 teaspoon thyme
- ¼ teaspoon black pepper
- 2 tablespoons butter, melted
- ¼ cup whole flour
- 2 cups cheddar cheese, shredded

DIRECTIONS

1. In a large saucepan, heat oil; add onions and cook over medium heat until softened for about 5 minutes.
2. Add broth, water, cauliflower, rosemary, thyme, and pepper. Cover; cook over low heat for 30 minutes, or until cauliflower is tender. Remove from heat.
3. Using a potato masher, mash the cauliflower mixture until it is broken into small pieces; return to heat.
4. In a small bowl, combine melted butter and flour; mix well, then add to soup, cooking over low heat and stirring until soup is thickened to desired consistency.
5. Add cheese, one cup at a time, stirring until cheese is melted. Serve.

NUTRITION

Calories: 252
Total Fat: 14g
Total Carbohydrate: 24g

Protein: 0g

25. Creamy Chicken Vegetable Soup

PREPARATION TIME
15'

COOK TIME
45'

SERVING
6

INGREDIENTS

- 2 tablespoons olive oil
- ½ cup onions, finely chopped
- ½ cup carrots, thinly sliced or shredded
- ½ cup potatoes, diced
- ½ cup green beans
- ½ cup peas
- 1 cup chicken, finely chopped
- 1 (14-ounce) can chicken broth
- ¼ teaspoon black pepper
- 1¼ cups milk
- 1 (10¾-ounce) can cream of celery soup
- 1 (10¾-ounce) can cream of cheddar cheese soup

DIRECTIONS

1. In a large saucepan, heat oil; add onions and carrots; cook and stir until softened, about 5 minutes.
2. Add potatoes, green beans, peas, chicken, broth, and pepper. Cover, and cook over low heat for 1½ hours, or until vegetables are soft; stir occasionally.
3. Add milk, celery soup and cheddar cheese soup; stir and continue cooking until heated throughout.

NUTRITION

Calories: 125
Total Fat: 3.6g
Total Carbohydrate: 15.6g

Protein: 7.6g

26. Clam Chowder

PREPARATION TIME
10'

COOK TIME
45'

SERVING
6

INGREDIENTS

- 1 cup onion, finely chopped
- 3 cups potatoes, diced
- 1 clove garlic, finely chopped
- 2 slices turkey bacon, cooked and finely crumbled
- 1 teaspoon salt
- ¼ teaspoon black pepper
- 1 (8-ounce) bottle clam juice
- 2 (7-ounce) cans minced clams
- 3 tablespoons whole flour
- 1 cup milk
- 2 cups half-and-half

DIRECTIONS

1. Remove starch from potatoes by slicing them and soaking in lukewarm water and straining 4 times.
2. In a large saucepan, combine onion, potatoes, garlic, turkey bacon, salt, pepper, and clam juice; cover and cook on low for 30 minutes, or until vegetables are soft.
3. In a small bowl, stir flour into milk; mix well.
4. Add flour and milk mixture to a saucepan along with half-and-half and clams with their liquid; stirring constantly, cook over medium heat until chowder thickens to desired consistency.
5. Transfer the mixture to a blender; blend until smooth and return to saucepan.

NUTRITION

Calories: 163
Total Fat: 5.83g
Total Carbohydrate: 19.01g

Protein: 8.83g

27. Cream of Broccoli Soup

PREPARATION TIME
10'

COOK TIME
45'

SERVING
6

INGREDIENTS

- 4 cups broccoli florets
- 1 cup onion, chopped
- 1 tablespoon celery flakes
- 1 clove garlic, chopped
- 1 medium potato, peeled and diced
- 1 (14-ounce) chicken broth
- 2 cups milk
- 1½ cups cheddar cheese, shredded
- ¼ teaspoon thyme
- ½ teaspoon salt
- ¼ teaspoon white pepper

DIRECTIONS

1. In a medium saucepan, add broccoli, onion, celery flakes, garlic, potato, and chicken broth; bring to near boiling; reduce heat, cover and cook over low heat for 30 minutes, or until vegetables are soft.
2. Transfer cooked vegetables with broth to a blender; blend until smooth.
3. Return blended vegetables to saucepan; add milk, cheese, thyme, salt, and pepper.
4. Continue cooking over low heat until cheese is melted, stirring constantly.

NUTRITION

Calories: 150
Total Fat: 7g
Total Carbohydrate: 15g

Protein: 5g

28. Chicken Noodle Soup

PREPARATION TIME
10'

COOK TIME
1h 30'

SERVING
6-8

INGREDIENTS

- 1 tablespoon olive or canola oil
- ¾ cup onion, finely chopped
- 2/3 cup carrots, shredded
- 4 cups chicken broth
- 2 cups water
- 1 tablespoon dried celery flakes
- 1 bay leaf
- 1 cup cooked chicken, finely chopped
- 1 tablespoon parsley flakes
- 1 teaspoon seasoned salt
- ¼ teaspoon black pepper, or to taste
- 1½ cups egg noodles, uncooked and broken into 3-inch pieces

DIRECTIONS

1. In a large saucepan, add oil, carrots and onion, then allow to cook on medium heat until soft, about 5 minutes.
2. Add broth, water, celery flakes, bay leaf, and chicken; cover and cook over low heat for 1 hour, stirring occasionally.
3. Stir in parsley, seasoned salt, pepper, and noodles; cover and continue cooking over low heat for 25 minutes. Remove bay leaf before serving.

NUTRITION

Calories: 220
Total Fat: 5g
Total Carbohydrate: 24g

Protein: 18g

29. Cream of Potato Soup

PREPARATION TIME
10'

COOK TIME
45'

SERVING
6

INGREDIENTS

- 1 tablespoon butter
- 1 cup onion, finely chopped
- 3 cups diced potatoes
- 3 cups chicken broth
- ¼ teaspoon black pepper
- ½ teaspoon salt
- ½ teaspoon garlic powder
- ¼ cup whole flour
- 1½ cups milk
- 1 cup sharp cheddar cheese, shredded (optional)

DIRECTIONS

1. In a medium saucepan, melt butter over medium heat. Add onion; stir and cook until onions are softened.
2. Add potatoes, chicken broth, pepper, salt, and garlic powder, plus ham if desired.
3. Cover; cook over low heat until potatoes are tender and easily fall apart for about 40 minutes.
4. In a small bowl, combine flour and milk; mix until smooth. Stir flour mixture into soup; continue cooking and stirring until soup is thickened and of desired consistency.
5. Add cheese if desired; stir just until melted and smooth. Serve.

NUTRITION

Calories: 225.7
Total Fat: 5.7g
Total Carbohydrate: 39g

Protein: 4.6g

30. Chicken and Bean Soup

PREPARATION TIME
10'

COOK TIME
40'

SERVING
2-4

INGREDIENTS

- 1 tablespoon olive oil
- ½ cup onion, finely chopped
- 1 clove garlic, finely chopped
- 1 (14½-ounce) can chicken broth, with roasted vegetable and herb flavoring
- ½ cup water
- 1 cup canned great northern beans, rinsed and drained
- ¾ cup chicken, cooked and finely chopped
- ¼ teaspoon black pepper
- 1 strip veggie bacon, cooked and finely crumbled

DIRECTIONS

1. In a medium saucepan, heat oil; add onion and garlic, cooking over low heat until softened, about 5 minutes.
2. Add broth and water to saucepan; bring to near boiling; reduce heat.
3. Add remaining ingredients; cover and cook over low heat for 30 minutes. Stir occasionally.

NUTRITION

Calories: 225.7
Total Fat: 5.7g
Total Carbohydrate: 39g

Protein: 4.6g

31. Chicken Ramen Soup Broth

PREPARATION TIME
10'

COOK TIME
1 hour

SERVING
2-3

INGREDIENTS

- 1 large onion, diced
- 2 carrots, diced
- 3 celery, diced
- 4 cloves garlic, finely chopped
- 1 tsp Kosher salt
- ½ tsp pepper
- 2 tsp Cinnamon
- 6 chicken broth, low sodium
- 2 tsp Light Miso
- 1 lb. chicken breasts
- 1 bag spinach

DIRECTIONS

1. Prepare carrots, celery, and onions for cooking in a latch Dutch oven for 5–7 minutes over medium heat. Now include salt, pepper, cinnamon, and garlic, and continue to cook for an additional minute.
2. Add chicken broth and miso before bringing to a boil.
3. Now add whole chicken breasts (raw), and simmer. Continue for 10–12 minutes. Occasionally remove a chicken breast and cut it, to see if it is cooked.
4. When the chicken is cooked thoroughly, relocate it to a cutting board for cooling.
5. When the chicken is cool enough to be handled, mince it finely, then add it back into the vegetable broth.
6. Stir in spinach to cook for approximately 5 minutes until spinach is tender.
7. Serve and enjoy!

NUTRITION

Calories: 326.9
Total Fat: 13.4 g
Total Carbohydrate: 39.7 g

Protein: 10.3 g

32. Carrot, Ginger Gusto Apple Soup

PREPARATION TIME
15′

COOK TIME
35′

SERVING
3

INGREDIENTS

- 2 cup yellow apple, chunks, peeled
- 1 cup boiled chicken, shredded
- 1 carrot, peeled and chopped
- ¼ cup cherries, chopped
- 2 cups chicken broth
- 1 tablespoon lemon juice
- 1 teaspoon ginger paste
- ½ teaspoon black pepper
- ¼ teaspoon salt
- 1 tablespoon oil

DIRECTIONS

1. Heat oil in a pan, add ginger paste and fry for 1 minute.
2. Add all chicken and carrots, then fry well.
3. Season with salt and pepper.
4. Transfer apple chunks, strawberries, chicken broth and stir well.
5. Place them to cook on low fire for 30 minutes.
6. Drizzle lemon juice.
7. Strain, and ladle into serving bowls.
8. Serve and enjoy.

NUTRITION

Calories: 172.3
Total Fat: 8.7 g
Total Carbohydrate: 22.7 g

Protein: 3.2 g

33. Carrot, Ginger Zest Chicken Orangey Soup 20

PREPARATION TIME
5'

COOK TIME
15'

SERVING
3

INGREDIENTS

- 1 oz. chicken bones or boiled chicken feet
- 2 oranges, sliced, seeded
- 2 carrots, peeled and chopped
- 2 cups chicken broth
- 1 teaspoon ginger paste
- ½ teaspoon chili powder
- ¼ teaspoon salt
- 1 tablespoon oil

DIRECTIONS

1. Heat oil in a pan, add ginger paste and carrot, then cook for 1 minute.
2. Add chicken, salt, chili powder and fry till golden brown.
3. Add chicken broth, orange slice and stir.
4. Leave to cook on low heat for 15 minutes.
5. Strain and ladle into serving bowls.
6. Serve and enjoy.

NUTRITION

Calories: 159
Total Fat: 3 g
Total Carbohydrate: 27 g

Protein: 6 g

34. Rice Cooker Garden Soup

PREPARATION TIME
10'

COOK TIME
50'

SERVING
6

INGREDIENTS

- 15oz. can chickpeas, rinsed and drained
- 2 carrots, diced
- 2 zucchinis, trimmed, cubed
- 2 sprigs thyme
- 1 leek, white and light green parts chopped
- ½ cup bulgur
- 4oz. green beans, cut into ½-inch pieces
- 6 cups water
- 2 garlic cloves, minced
- 2 cups chicken stock
- 2 tablespoons butter
- 1 cup tomatoes, chopped
- 1 cup fresh peas
- 1 bay leaf
- Salt and pepper, to taste

DIRECTIONS

1. Set your rice cooker to white rice.
2. Add the butter and once melted add the celery, chickpeas, leek, garlic, zucchinis, garlic.
3. Cook, stirring for 4 minutes.
4. Add the stock, bulgur, tomatoes, bay leaf, water, and thyme.
5. Simmer for 30 minutes. Add the green beans and peas. Discard the thyme. Cook for 5 minutes.
6. Serve after.

NUTRITION

Calories: 100
Total Fat: 3.5 g
Total Carbohydrate: 18 g

Protein: 3 g

35. Lemony Chicken Soup Broth

PREPARATION TIME
10'

COOK TIME
1 hour

SERVING
2-3

INGREDIENTS

- 1 Onion, large, diced
- 2 Carrots, diced
- 3 Celery, diced
- 4 cloves garlic, finely chopped
- 1 tsp Kosher salt
- ½ tsp pepper
- 2 tsp Cinnamon
- 6 Chicken broth, low sodium
- 10 sprigs Parsley, extra for garnish

- 1 lb. Chicken breasts
- 1 bag Spinach
- 15 ounces chickpeas, canned, washed/drained
- Juice of a Lemon (½ lemon, or more to taste)

DIRECTIONS

1. Prepare carrots, celery, and onions for cooking in a latch Dutch oven for 5–7 minutes over medium heat. Now include salt, pepper, cinnamon, and garlic, and continue to cook for an additional minute.
2. Add whole parsley sprigs to your pot and stir in chicken broth before bringing it to a boil.
3. Now add whole chicken breasts (raw), and simmer. Continue for 10–12 minutes. Occasionally remove a chicken breast and cut it, to see if it is cooked.
4. When the chicken is cooked thoroughly, relocate it to a cutting board for cooling.
5. When the chicken is cool enough to be handled, shred it, then add it back into the vegetable broth.
6. Stir in lemon juice, chickpeas, and spinach to cook for approximately 5 minutes until spinach is tender.
7. Strain the soup to gather the broth and discard the solids, garnish with newly chopped parsley, and enjoy!

NUTRITION

Calories: 252.8
Total Fat: 8 g
Total Carbohydrate: 19.8 g

Protein: 25.6 g

36. Super Soup

PREPARATION TIME
10'

COOK TIME
30'

SERVING
6

INGREDIENTS

- 14oz. cauliflower heat, cut into florets
- 5oz. watercress
- 7oz. spinach, thawed
- 4 cups chicken stock
- 1 cup coconut milk
- ¼ cup ghee
- Salt and pepper—to taste
- 1 onion, chopped
- 2 garlic cloves, crushed

DIRECTIONS

1. Grease Dutch oven with ghee, place over medium-high heat and add onion and garlic. Cook until browned and stir cauliflower florets. Cook for 5 minutes.
2. Add spinach and watercress and cook for 2 minutes or until just wilted, pour in vegetable stock and bring to boil.
3. Cook until cauliflower is crisp-tender and stir in the coconut milk.
4. Season with salt and pepper and remove from the heat. Allow cooling and puree the soup in NutriBullet until creamy.
5. Strain through a fine sieve or cheesecloth and serve immediately.

NUTRITION

Calories: 392
Total Fat: 37.6 g
Total Carbohydrate: 9.7 g

Protein: 4.9 g

37. Tomato bisque

PREPARATION TIME
10'

COOK TIME
30'

SERVING
4

INGREDIENTS

- 28 oz. tomatoes, peeled and pureed
- 1 cup coconut cream
- 1 onion, diced
- 1 teaspoon fresh ground pepper
- 4 cups chicken stock
- 1 bunch celery, chopped
- ½ cup basil, chopped
- 1 tablespoon olive oil
- Salt and pepper—to taste

DIRECTIONS

1. Heat olive oil in a large pot over medium-high heat, add onion, with celery and cook until tender.
2. Pour chicken stock and tomatoes in the pot, bring mixture to simmer and season with salt and pepper. Simmer for 30 minutes.
3. Turn off the heat and allow the soup to cool down. Puree in NutriBullet in batches.
4. Stir in heavy cream, basil, and Parmesan cheese.
5. Strain through a fine sieve or cheesecloth and serve immediately.

NUTRITION

Calories: 140
Total Fat: 7 g
Total Carbohydrate: 17 g

Protein: 3 g

38. Smoky Soup V

PREPARATION TIME
15'

COOK TIME
40'

SERVING
4

INGREDIENTS

- 3 red bell peppers, diced
- 1 ½ tablespoons grass-fed butter
- 2 carrots, grated
- 1 brown onion, diced
- 2 garlic cloves, minced
- 1 ½ tablespoon tomato puree
- 2 teaspoons fresh grated ginger
- 1 teaspoon smoked paprika
- 1 bay leaf
- ½ cup chilled coconut cream whisked with 1 tablespoon lemon juice
- 4 cups homemade vegetable stock
- ½ teaspoon ground coriander

DIRECTIONS

1. Melt butter in a medium heavy-bottom pan, over medium-high heat.
2. Add carrots, bell peppers, and onion. Cook for 13–15 minutes or until onion is golden, stirring occasionally.
3. Add garlic, ginger, smoked paprika, tomato puree and coriander.
4. Cook until very fragrant, for 2 minutes.
5. Add bay leaf and stock; bring to boil and reduce heat to medium-low and simmer for 20v25 minutes.
6. Remove bay leaf and when cooled puree in batches using NutriBullet. Process until smooth.
7. Stir Strain in a fine sieve or cheesecloth and serve immediately.

NUTRITION

Calories: 100
Total Fat: 2 g
Total Carbohydrate: 16 g

Protein: 5 g

39. Onion and Peas Soup

PREPARATION TIME
10'

COOK TIME
25'

SERVING
3

INGREDIENTS

- 1 cup peas, boiled
- 2 carrots, peeled, chopped
- 1 onion, sliced
- 2 cups chicken broth
- 1 tablespoon lemon juice
- 4–5 garlic cloves, minced
- ½ teaspoon black pepper
- ¼ teaspoon salt
- 1 tablespoon oil

DIRECTIONS

1. Heat oil in a saucepan, add onion and garlic cloves, fry for 2 minutes.
2. Add all peas and carrots stir for 5 minutes.
3. Add chicken broth, salt, pepper, and mix well.
4. Leave to cook on low heat for 15 minutes.
5. Strain and ladle into serving bowls.
6. Drizzle lemon juice.
7. Serve and enjoy.

NUTRITION

Calories: 115

Total Fat: 0 g

Total Carbohydrate: 21 g

Protein: 7 g

40. Curried Carrot, Sweet Potato, and Ginger Soup V

PREPARATION TIME
10'

COOK TIME
35'

SERVING
3

INGREDIENTS

- 2 tsp. Extra Virgin Olive Oil
- ½ cup Shallots, chopped
- 3 cups Sweet Potato, peeled, cubed
- 1½ cup Carrots, peeled, sliced

DIRECTIONS

1. Place a saucepan with your oil on medium heat until it just begins to smoke.
2. Add your shallots to the pot and sauté until it becomes tender (should take approximately 2–3 min).
3. Add all your prepped vegetables to the shallots, and your curry then allow to cook for another 2 minutes.
4. Pour in your broth and allow it to come to a boil. Once boiling, place the lid on the pot and reduce the heat to low.
5. Allow this mixture to simmer until your vegetables are all tender.
6. Once tender, add salt and pour your soup into a food processor. Pulse until creamy and smooth.
7. Strain, serve and Enjoy.

Tip: Consider topping with a teaspoon of vanilla Greek yogurt and sesame seeds.

NUTRITION

Calories: 144
Total Fat: 2.3 g
Total Carbohydrate: 27.3 g

Protein: 4.1 g

CHAPTER 6
Breakfast

41. Lettuce Power Pack

PREPARATION TIME
15'

COOK TIME
15'

SERVING
1

INGREDIENTS

- 1 egg, large
- 1 white of an egg, large
- 125 ml baby spinach leaves, small pieces
- 2 tbsp. fat-free feta, crumbled
- 2 tomatoes, roam, small pieces
- Pinch of salt, kosher or sea
- Black pepper
- 1 large lettuce leaf, preferably not iceberg

DIRECTIONS

1. Place the first seven ingredients in a bowl and whisk well.
2. Have a nonstick pan heating on medium heat, add the combined mixture, and cook to the consistency of your choice.
3. Place the cooked ingredients on one end of the leaf and roll up.

NUTRITION

Calories: 52
Total Fat: 2.9g
Total Carbohydrate: 5.6g

Protein: 1.1g

42. Greek Egg Muffins

PREPARATION TIME
5'

COOK TIME
10'

SERVING
6

INGREDIENTS

Can be made ahead and enjoyed throughout the week for breakfast or lunch.

- 5 eggs large
- 10 cherry tomatoes, quartered
- 5 artichoke hearts, marinated and diced
- 125 ml mozzarella cheese, low-fat and shredded
- 2 tbsp. basil, fresh and minced
- Pepper and salt for taste
- Cooking time spray for the muffin tin

DIRECTIONS

1. While the oven is preheating to 350°F, break the eggs into a bowl and whisk well until smooth.
2. Combine the rest of the ingredients with the eggs and stir gently together.
3. Coat the muffin tin cups lightly with the cooking time spray.
4. Spoon the egg mixture into six cups, dividing it equally.
5. Bake for twenty min or 'til the eggs is set.
6. Let cool for a minute before savoring or store in the fridge to be enjoyed later.

NUTRITION

Calories: 106
Fats: 6g
Protein: 10g

43. Sunday Morning Special

PREPARATION TIME
20'

COOK TIME
10'

SERVING
1

INGREDIENTS

- 125 ml cottage cheese, low fat
- 1 egg, large
- 75 ml onion diced
- 1/4 tsp garlic minced
- 1 generous tbsp. whole wheat flour
- Pepper and salt for taste
- Cooking time spray for the pan

DIRECTIONS

1. Spray the pan and pre-heat for a minute.
2. Sauté the garlic and onions, while stirring together the egg, cottage cheese, flour and pepper, and salt.
3. Add the cooked ingredients to the bowl mixture, stirring until well-combined.
4. Spray the pan again and spoon in the mixture to the pan. Create 4 pancakes.
5. Cook on each side for four min.

NUTRITION

Protein: 36 g
Fat: 96 g
Carbohydrates: 10 g

44. Simple Sunshine Scramble

PREPARATION TIME
5'

COOK TIME
10'

SERVING
1

INGREDIENTS

- 1 egg
- 1 clove garlic, small minced
- 1 tsp pesto
- 2 cherry tomatoes, quartered
- 1-piece bacon turkey, crumbled
- 1 tsp parmesan cheese, grated fine
- Cooking time spray for the pan

DIRECTIONS

1. Lightly whisk the egg in a mixing bowl. Add a dash of water to the egg and the pesto. Whisk again lightly.
2. Spray the pan lightly with cooking time spray and heat to medium-high.
3. Sauté the garlic until the aroma is released. Stir in bacon to crisp.
4. Slide pan contents out onto a side dish. Add tomatoes to the pan, sauté until the liquid is almost gone. Add egg mixture to the pan and cook as for how you prefer your scrambled eggs. Stir in the bacon/garlic mixture and parmesan cheese just before the eggs are cooked. Serve it with a slice of orange for that complete sunshine feel.

NUTRITION

Protein: 60 g
Fat: 144 g
Carbohydrates: 8 g

45. Black Beans Puree with Scrambled Eggs

PREPARATION TIME
20'

COOK TIME
30'

SERVING
1

INGREDIENTS

For making the scrambled egg part of the recipe:
- 1/8 teaspoon salt
- 1 egg
- 1/8 teaspoon pepper
- 1/8 cup of Black beans puree

- 3 tablespoons enchilada sauce (green)
- 1/2 cup rinsed black beans
- 2 tablespoon vegetable or chicken broth
- 1 tablespoon protein powder

DIRECTIONS

Black beans puree:
1. Put the beans in a small-sized saucepan on medium heat. Then put the enchilada sauce. Heat for 2 min. Keep stirring all the time. Then add the chicken broth.
2. Shift the mixture to one blender or use one hand blender to make a smooth mixture. Transfer it into one bowl.
3. Let it cool a bit and then mix the protein powder. Stir well. Cover it to keep it warm till you cook the egg.
4. Keep the leftovers in the fridge so that you can eat them at some other time.

Scrambled egg:
5. Heat one non-stick pan on medium heat. In the meantime, put the egg in one small bowl and whisk it well to incorporate air into it.
6. Pour the egg into the heated pan. Sprinkle pepper and salt. Use one rubber spatula for moving the egg in the pan while it is getting cooked. When it is almost done and still has a slightly liquid texture, you should fold it and take it out on a plate.
7. Put 1 tablespoon of the black beans puree. Also, put 1 teaspoon of enchilada sauce (green).

Note: It provides approximately 5 grams of fat, 11 grams of proteins, and 6 grams of carbohydrates.

NUTRITION

Calories: 52
Total Fat: 2.9g
Total Carbohydrate: 5.6g

Protein: 1.1g

46. Veggie Quiche Muffins

PREPARATION TIME
20'

COOK TIME
30'

SERVING
12

INGREDIENTS

- ¾ c. Shredded cheddar
- 1c. Green onion
- 1 c. Chopped broccoli
- 1 c. Diced tomatoes
- 2 c. Milk
- 4 eggs
- 1 pc. Pancake mix
- 1 tsp. Oregano
- ½ tsp. salt
- ½ tsp. pepper

DIRECTIONS

1. Set oven to 375°F, and lightly grease a 12-cup muffin tin with oil.
2. Sprinkle tomatoes, broccoli, onions and cheddar into muffin cups.
3. Combine remaining ingredients in a medium bowl, whisk to combine then pour evenly on top of veggies.
4. Set to bake in preheated oven for about 40 min or until golden brown.
5. Allow cooling slightly (about 5 min) then servings. Enjoy!

NUTRITION

Calories: 58.8
Fat: 3.2g
Carbs: 2.9g

Protein: 5.1g

47. Steel-cut Oat Blueberry Pancakes

PREPARATION TIME
10'

COOK TIME
10'

SERVING
4

INGREDIENTS

- 1½ c. Water
- ½ c. Oats
- 1/8 tsp. salt
- 1 c. Flour
- ½ tsp. Baking powder
- ½ tsp. Baking soda
- 1 egg
- 1 c. Milk
- ½ c. Greek yogurt
- 1 c. Frozen blueberries
- ¾ c. Agave nectar

DIRECTIONS

1. Combine oats, salt, and water together in a medium saucepan, stir, and allow to come to a boil over high heat.
2. Set it to low and simmer for 10 min, or until oats are tender. Set aside.
3. Combine all remaining ingredients, except agave nectar, in a medium bowl, then fold in oats.
4. Preheat griddle and lightly grease. Cook ¼ cup of batter at a time for about 3 min per side. Garnish with agave.

NUTRITION

Calories: 257
Fat: 7g
Carbs: 46g

Protein: 14g

48. Very Berry Muesli

PREPARATION TIME
2 hours

COOK TIME
4 hours

SERVING
2

INGREDIENTS

- 1 c. Oats
- 1 c. Fruit flavored yogurt
- ½ c. Milk
- 1/8 tsp. salt
- ½ c. Dried raisins
- ½ c. Chopped apple
- ½ c. Frozen blueberries
- ¼ c. Chopped walnuts

DIRECTIONS

1. Combine yogurt, salt and oats together in a medium bowl, mix well, then cover the mixture tightly.
2. Place in the refrigerator to cool for 6 hours.
3. Add raisins, and apples the gently fold.
4. Top with walnuts and servings. Enjoy!

NUTRITION

Calories: 198
Carbs: 31.2g
Fat: 4.3g

Protein: 6g

49. Strawberry & Mushroom Breakfast Sandwich

PREPARATION TIME
5'

COOK TIME
5'

SERVING
4

INGREDIENTS

- 8 oz. Cream cheese
- 1 tbsp. Honey
- 1 tbsp. Grated lemon zest
- 4 sliced Portobello mushrooms
- 2 c. Sliced strawberries

DIRECTIONS

1. Add honey, lemon zest and cheese to a food processor, and process until fully incorporated.
2. Use cheese mixture to spread on mushrooms as you would butter.
3. Top with strawberries. Enjoy!

NUTRITION

Calories: 180
Fat: 16g
Carbs: 6g

Protein: 2g

50. Shakshuka Egg Bake

PREPARATION TIME
10'

COOK TIME
30'

SERVING
4

INGREDIENTS

- 1 teaspoon extra-virgin olive oil
- ½ onion, minced
- 1 garlic clove, minced
- ½ teaspoon smoked paprika
- ½ teaspoon ground cumin
- 1 (15-ounce) can diced tomatoes

- 2 ounces feta cheese, crumbled
- 4 large eggs

DIRECTIONS

1. Preheat the oven to 350°F.
2. In a medium skillet over medium heat, heat the oil. Add the onions and garlic, and sauté until translucent, about 5 min. Add the paprika and cumin, and cook a minute longer.
3. Stir in the tomatoes until well combined. Simmer until some of their liquid has evaporated and the mixture begins to thicken to form a sauce, 5 to 10 min.
4. Divide the sauce evenly among 4 ramekins, and repeat with the cheese, sprinkling evenly across.
5. Using a spoon, create wells in the tomato sauce and crack an egg over each, being careful to keep the yolk intact.
6. Bake in the ramekins for 15 min, until the yolk is done to your liking, longer if you like a hard-cooked yolk, and serve. (If you do not have ramekins, crack the eggs into spoon-made wells in the pan and let cook for 5 to 10 min, or per your preference.)
7. Ingredient tip: For a variation on flavor, add diced bell pepper, chopped spinach, or chili powder.

NUTRITION

Calories: 144
Total fat: 9g
Protein: 9g

Carbohydrates: 7g
Fiber: 1g
Sugar: 4g

Sodium: 455mg.

51. Ricotta Baked in the Oven

PREPARATION TIME
10'

COOK TIME
30'

SERVING
4

INGREDIENTS

- 1/4th cup parmesan cheese (grated)
- 1/2 cup ricotta cheese (low fat)
- 1 teaspoon Dijon mustard
- 1 teaspoon thyme (ground)
- 1/4th cup cheddar cheese (shredded)
- 1 egg

DIRECTIONS

1. Heat the oven to a temperature of 400°F.
2. Put all the ingredients in one bowl. Stir and mix them well. The mixture will appear to be gritty and slightly brown. But it must be smooth.
3. Use one cookie scoop and divide the mixture into 4 wells of the muffin pan. You can use muffin pans made of silicone as you can use them easily and clean them quickly.
4. Bake it for about 20 min. Then remove from the oven and let it cool a bit. It is ready to be servings.

Note: This recipe is for making four ricotta muffins. Every muffin provides approximately 4 grams of fat, 4 grams of carbohydrates and 8 grams of proteins

NUTRITION

Calories: 124
Total fat: 4g
Protein: 8g

Carbohydrates: 4g
Fiber: 0.9g
Sugar: 2g

Sodium: 155mg.

52. Poached Eggs Italian Style

PREPARATION TIME
10'

COOK TIME
10'

SERVING
4

INGREDIENTS

- 3 to 4 pieces of jarred red pepper (roasted and sliced)
- 16 oz. of marinara sauce (with the lowest level of sugar)
- 4 eggs
- 4 leaves fresh basil
- 1 pinch salt
- 1 pinch pepper

DIRECTIONS

1. Heat a big, rimmed skillet on medium heat. Put the marinara sauce. Then add the red peppers. Crack the eggs one by one making a "well" with the back of one spoon. Sprinkle pepper and salt.
2. Allow it to cook till the eggs become firm or for around 12 min. If you'd like you can put the lid for 2 min at the end.
3. Remove from the heat. Sprinkle basil and serving in a bowl or plate.

NUTRITION

Fat: 6 g
Proteins: 8 g
Carbohydrates: 7 g

53. Denver Egg Muffins with Ham Crust

PREPARATION TIME
15'

COOK TIME
30'

SERVING
12

INGREDIENTS

- Nonstick cooking time spray
- 12 slices deli ham
- ½ cup cheddar cheese
- 1 teaspoon extra-virgin olive oil
- ½ onion, diced
- ½ green pepper, minced
- 10 large eggs
- ¼ cup low-fat milk

DIRECTIONS

1. Preheat the oven to 350°F.
2. Grease a 12-compartment muffin tin with cooking time spray.
3. Line each cup with a ham slice, pushing it down to fit tightly against the edge of the well.
4. In a small skillet over medium heat, heat the oil. Add the onion and green pepper, and sauté for 3 min, or until soft. Remove from the heat, and drain any liquid from the pan.
5. In a large bowl, whisk the eggs and milk. Add the cheese and cooked vegetables, and whisk again.
6. Ladle ¼ cup of the egg mixture into each cup. If there is any left over, divide evenly among the cups.
7. Bake for 20 to 25 min, or just until the eggs are firm and no longer runny, and servings.

Ingredient tip: Switch things up, and be creative with your vegetables, meat, and cheese. Try broccoli and cheddar, sundried tomato and feta, or sausage with pepper jack cheese. Garnish with hot sauce, salsa, avocado, herbs, or light sour cream.

NUTRITION

Calories: 99
Total fat: 6g
Protein: 8g

Carbohydrates: 1g
Fiber: 0g
Sugar: 1g

Sodium: 206mg

54. Cheesy Slow Cooker Egg Casserole

PREPARATION TIME
15'

COOK TIME
4-8 hours

SERVING
8

INGREDIENTS

- 1-pound fresh Italian chicken sausage
- Nonstick cooking time spray
- 1 (30-ounce) bag frozen hash browns
- 1 medium red bell pepper, seeded and diced
- ½ medium onion, diced
- 1 (4-ounce) can mild diced green chiles
- 1½ cups low-fat shredded cheddar

- cheese, divided into three ½-cup
- 12 large eggs
- 1 cup low-fat milk
- ½ teaspoon salt
- ½ teaspoon freshly ground black pepper

DIRECTIONS

1. Remove the casings from the sausage, and discard.
2. In a large skillet over medium heat, brown the meat, breaking into smaller pieces as it cooks, about 7 min, or until no longer pink.
3. Spray a 5-quart slow cooker with nonstick cooking time spray, and layer half of the frozen hash browns, cooked sausage, pepper, onion, and chiles, plus ½ cup of cheese. Repeat with the remaining hash browns, sausage, pepper, onion, and chiles, plus another ½ cup of cheese.
4. In a large bowl, whisk the eggs, milk, salt, and pepper.
5. Pour the egg mixture over the potato-sausage layers, and top with the remaining ½ cup of cheese.
6. Cook on high for 4 hours or on low for 8 hours, and servings.

Ingredient tip: If you cannot find fresh Italian chicken sausage, look for precooked sausage in the refrigerator section of your grocery store. Dice into small pieces and brown in a skillet before adding to the slow cooker.

NUTRITION

Calories: 348
Total fat: 17g
Protein: 27g

Carbohydrates: 24g
Fiber: 3g
Sugar: 3g

Sodium: 783mg

55. Make-ahead Breakfast Burritos

PREPARATION TIME
15'

COOK TIME
20'

SERVING
8

INGREDIENTS

- 12 large eggs
- ¼ cup low-fat milk
- 1 teaspoon extra-virgin olive oil
- ½ medium yellow onion, diced
- 1 medium green bell pepper, seeded and diced
- 1 cup canned black beans, drained and rinsed
- 8 (7- to 8-inch) whole wheat tortillas
- ½ cup shredded cheddar cheese
- 8 ounces salsa

DIRECTIONS

1. In a large bowl, whisk together the eggs and milk.
2. In a large skillet over medium heat, heat the oil. Add the onion, bell pepper, and black beans. Sauté until the onion is translucent, about 5 min, and transfer to a plate.
3. Pour the egg mixture into the skillet, and gently stir until the eggs are fluffy and firm. Remove from the heat.
4. Divide the eggs and onion mixture evenly among the tortillas, and top with the cheese and salsa.
5. With both sides of the first tortilla tucked in, roll tightly to close. Repeat with the remaining tortillas.
6. Serve immediately, or freeze for up to 3 months. If freezing, wrap the burritos in paper towels and cover them tightly with aluminum foil for storage.
7. Post-op Serving: suggestions
8. Ingredient tip: if you cannot tolerate doughy textures after surgery, skip the tortilla and spoon the filling in a bowl.

NUTRITION

Calories: 264
Total fat: 12g
Protein: 21g

Carbohydrates: 24g
Fiber: 11g
Sugar: 3g

Sodium: 593mg

56. Baked Broccoli and Eggs

PREPARATION TIME
10'

COOK TIME
15'

SERVING
1

INGREDIENTS

- 4 ounces Margarine, light
- 10 ounces Broccoli, frozen, thawed, chopped
- 4 ounces Pimento, jarred, chopped
- 6 tablespoons Flour
- 1 dash Black pepper, freshly ground
- 1/2 cup Mushrooms, sliced, fresh
- 6 pieces Eggs, large
- 1/2-pound Cheddar cheese, low fat
- 2 pounds Cottage cheese, nonfat
- 1 teaspoon salt
- 1 dash Paprika

DIRECTIONS

1. Set the oven to 350°F to preheat.
2. Meanwhile, place the eggs, broccoli, and all other ingredients in a large bowl. Stir to combine.
3. Use cooking time spray to coat the sides and bottom of a casserole dish (2-quart).
4. Fill the preparation time dish with the broccoli-egg mixture, making sure to spread it evenly.
5. Bake in the oven for one hour and thirty min.
6. Serve immediately.

NUTRITION

Calories: 129
Carbohydrates: 2g
Protein: 10g
Fat: 9g

Saturated fat: 4g
Cholesterol: 179mg
Sodium: 218mg
Potassium: 113mg

Fiber: 1g
Sugar: 2g
Vitamin a: 363iu
Vitamin c: 1mg

Calcium: 142mg
Iron: 1mg

57. Black Bean and Pumpkin Soup

PREPARATION TIME
5'

COOK TIME
15'

SERVING
2 cups

INGREDIENTS

- 1-piece Onion, medium, chopped
- 1/2 teaspoon Black pepper, freshly ground
- 16 ounces pumpkin puree, canned
- 1 tablespoon Cumin, ground
- 1 cup Tomatoes, canned, diced
- 2 tablespoons Olive oil, extra virgin
- 4 pieces Garlic cloves, minced
- 4 pieces Chili powder
- 30 ounces Black beans, canned, rinsed, drained
- 2 cups Beef broth, low sodium

DIRECTIONS

1. Heat a soup kettle on medium after filling with the oil.
2. Add the garlic, onions, pepper, chili powder, and cumin. Stir and cook for about two to three min or until soft and fragrant.
3. Add the broth as well as pumpkin, tomatoes, and black beans. Stir to combine.
4. Allow the mixture to simmer, uncovered, for twenty-five min or until thickened to your desired consistency.
5. Remove from heat and process the black bean and pumpkin soup with an immersion blender.
6. Serve and enjoy.

NUTRITION

Calories: 266
Carbohydrates: 13g
Protein: 4g
Fat: 24g

Saturated fat: 21g
Sodium: 879mg
Potassium: 641mg
Fiber: 3g

Sugar: 4g
Vitamin a: 17726iu
Vitamin c: 23mg
Calcium: 71mg

Iron: 6mg

58. Broccoli and Tofu Quiche

PREPARATION TIME
10'

COOK TIME
15'

SERVING
3

INGREDIENTS

- 1/4 teaspoon salt
- 1/4 pound mushrooms, chopped
- 1 tablespoon pickled plum/white miso paste
- 1-piece yellow onion, chopped
- 2 tablespoons sesame tahini

- 1/2 cup Bulgur wheat, uncooked
- 1 tablespoon Sesame oil
- 1/2-pound Broccoli, chopped
- 1 ½ pounds Tofu
- 1 tablespoon Tamari

DIRECTIONS

1. Set the oven at 350°F to preheat.
2. Fill a small pot with water (1 cup) and heat on medium. Bring to a boil before adding in the bulgur and salt. Stir to combine and allow the mixture to boil again. Reduce heat to low and cover to cook for about fifteen min.
3. Meanwhile, grease a pie pan (9-inch) with a little oil. Pour the cooked bulgur into the pie pan, pressing lightly to spread it evenly at the bottom. Place in the oven to bake for about twelve min or until crusty on top. Let stand to cool.
4. Heat a large skillet (nonstick) on medium-high before adding the onions. Stir in the mushrooms and broccoli and cook for two min. Cover and immediately remove from heat.
5. Meanwhile, fill the food processor with tofu. Add the tamari, tahini, and umeboshi paste. Process until well-combined and smooth, then pour into a large bowl.
6. Add the cooked veggies and gently toss until evenly coated. Transfer the veggie mixture onto the crusted bulgur. Bake in the oven for about half an hour. Once done, let stand on a wire rack. After ten min, slice into 6 portions and serve: immediately.

NUTRITION

Calories: 248
Carbohydrates: 27.2g
Protein: 30.6g

Fat: 3.6g
Saturated fat: 0.4g
Cholesterol: 50mg

Sodium: 718mg
Fiber: 6.1g

59. Cheese-filled Acorn Squash

PREPARATION TIME
10'

COOK TIME
50'

SERVING
3

INGREDIENTS

- 1-pound Tofu, firm
- 1 teaspoon Basil
- 1 pinch Black pepper, freshly ground
- 1 teaspoon Onion, chopped finely
- 1 teaspoon Garlic powder
- 1 cup Cheddar cheese, reduced fat, shredded

- 2 pieces Acorn squash, halved, seeded
- 1 cup Celery, diced
- 1 cup Mushrooms, fresh, sliced
- 1 teaspoon Oregano
- 1/8 teaspoon salt
- 8 ounces Tomato sauce

DIRECTIONS

1. Set the oven at 350°F to preheat.
2. Arrange the acorn squash pieces, with their cut-sides facing down, at the bottom of a glass dish.
3. Place in the microwave oven and cook for about twenty min or until softened. Set aside.
4. Heat a saucepan (nonstick) on medium, then add the tofu (sliced into cubes). Cook until browned before stirring in the onion and celery. Cook for two min or until the onion is translucent.
5. Add the mushrooms. Stir to combine and cook for an additional two to three min. Pour in the tomato sauce as well as the dry seasonings.
6. Give everything a good stir, then spoon equal portions of the mixture inside the acorn squash pieces.
7. Cover and place in the oven to cook for about fifteen min. Uncover and top with the cheese before returning to the oven. Cook for five more min or until the cheese is melted and bubbling. Serve immediately.

NUTRITION

Calories: 328
Carbohydrates: 47.5g
Protein: 16.9g
Fat: 10.8g

Saturated fat: 5.8g
Polyunsaturated fat: 5g
Cholesterol: 42mg
Sodium: 557mg

Fiber: 7.7g
Sugar: 5.9g

60. Cheesy Spinach Bake

PREPARATION TIME
5'

COOK TIME
35'

SERVING
4

INGREDIENTS

- 2 pieces Eggs, whole
- 1/2 cup Parmesan cheese
- 2 cups Cottage cheese, fat-free/low fat
- 10 ounces Spinach, frozen, thawed, drained

DIRECTIONS

1. Set the oven to 350°F to preheat. Meanwhile, line a baking pan (8x8) with parchment paper.
2. Place all ingredients in a large bowl. Stir to combine. Pour the cheesy spinach mixture into the preparation time bedpan. Place in the oven to bake for twenty to thirty min or until the cheese on top is bubbling.
3. Remove from the oven and allow to cool for five min.
4. Serve sprinkled with garlic, salt, and pepper. Enjoy.

NUTRITION

Calories: 292
Carbohydrates: 4.5g
Protein: 26g fat: 19.1g

Saturated fat: 7.2g
Monounsaturated fat: 11.9g
Cholesterol: 545mg

Sodium: 735mg
Fiber: 2g

61. Southwestern Scrambled Egg Burritos

PREPARATION TIME
100'

COOK TIME
10'

SERVING
8

INGREDIENTS

- 12 eggs
- ¼ cup low-fat milk
- 1 teaspoon extra-virgin olive oil
- ½ onion, chopped
- 1 red bell pepper, diced
- 1 green bell pepper, diced
- 1 (15-ounce) can of black beans, drained and rinsed
- 8 (7-8 inch) whole-wheat tortillas, such as La Tortilla Factory low-carb tortillas
- 1 cup salsa, for serving

DIRECTIONS

1. Using a big bowl stir the eggs and milk. Set aside.
2. In a large skillet over medium-high heat, heat the olive oil and add the onion and bell peppers. Sauté for 2 to 3 minutes, or until tender. Add the beans and stir to combine.
3. Add the egg mixture. Minimize heat and mix while constantly with a rubber spatula for 5 minutes, until the eggs are fluffy and cooked through.
4. Divide the scrambled egg mixture among the tortillas. Fold over the bottom end of the tortilla, fold in the sides, and roll tightly to close.
5. Serve immediately with the salsa, or place each burrito in a zip-top bag and refrigerate for up to 1 week. To eat, reheat each burrito in the microwave for 60 to 90 seconds. These will also keep well in the freezer for up to 1 month.
6. Serving tip: To get more vegetables into your breakfast, buy a bag of frozen California-blend mixed vegetables. Heat some in a skillet with extra-virgin olive oil, add eggs, and—voilà!—a quick veggie-packed egg burrito.

NUTRITION

Calories: 250
Total fat: 10g
Protein: 19g

Carbs: 28g
Fiber: 13g
Sugar: 1g

Sodium: 546mg

62. Smoothie Bowl with Greek Yogurt and Fresh Berries

PREPARATION TIME
5'

COOK TIME
5'

SERVING
1

INGREDIENTS

- ¾ cup unsweetened vanilla almond milk or low-fat milk
- ¼ cup low-fat plain Greek yogurt
- ⬚ cup (1 handful) fresh spinach
- ½ scoop (1/8 cup) plain or vanilla protein powder
- ¼ cup frozen mixed berries
- ¼ cup fresh raspberries
- ¼ cup fresh blueberries
- 1 tablespoon sliced, slivered almonds
- 1 teaspoon chia seeds

DIRECTIONS

1. In a blender, combine the milk, yogurt, spinach, protein powder, and frozen berries. For 4 minutes blend, until the powder is well dissolved and no longer visible.
2. Pour the smoothie into a small bowl.
3. Decorate the smoothie with raspberries, blueberries, almonds, and chia seeds.
4. Serve with a spoon and enjoy!

Serving tip: You can make this smoothie bowl with a variety of other fruits and toppings to change it up. Try a mango-pineapple version. Top with unsweetened, flaked coconut and use coconut milk in the smoothie base for a more tropical vibe.

NUTRITION

Calories: 255
Total fat: 10 g
Protein: 20g

Carbs: 21g
Fiber: 8g
Sugar: 10g

Sodium: 262mg

63. Cherry-Vanilla Baked Oatmeal

PREPARATION TIME
10'

COOK TIME
45'

SERVING
6

INGREDIENTS

- Nonstick cooking spray
- 1 cup old-fashioned oats
- ½ teaspoon ground cinnamon
- ¾ teaspoon baking powder
- 1 tablespoon ground flaxseed
- 3 eggs
- 1 cup low-fat milk
- ½ cup low-fat plain Greek yogurt
- 1 teaspoon vanilla extract
- 1 teaspoon liquid stevia (optional; to improve sweetness)
- 1 cup fresh pitted cherries
- 1 apple, peeled, cored and chopped

DIRECTIONS

1. Preheat the oven to 375°F. Lightly coat an 8-by-8-inch baking dish with the cooking spray.
2. Mix together the oats, cinnamon, baking powder, and flaxseed in a medium bowl. In a separate large bowl, gently whisk the eggs, milk, yogurt, vanilla, and stevia (if using).
3. Combine the dry ingredients and mix to combine. Gently fold in the cherries and apples.
4. Bake for 45 minutes or until the edges start to pull away from the side of the pan and the oatmeal gently bounces back when touched.
5. Divide leftover oatmeal into airtight glass containers. Refrigerate for up to 1 week for a quick and easy breakfast, or freeze.
6. Serving tip: Experiment with the fixings in your baked oatmeal. I like to make my recipes seasonal. Replace the yogurt with pumpkin puree to add a hint of fall. Try using unsweetened dried cranberries instead of cherries for a holiday twist. Swap out apples and cherries for 2 cups of fresh berries in spring for a very berry oatmeal! For the creamiest consistency, I recommend topping with a ¼ cup low-fat milk at serving time.

NUTRITION

Calories: 149

Total fat: 4g

Protein: 8g

Carbs: 21g

Fiber: 4g

Sugar: 9g

Sodium: 71 mg

64. High-Protein Pancakes

PREPARATION TIME
5'

COOK TIME
15'

SERVING
4

INGREDIENTS

- 3 eggs
- 1 cup low-fat cottage cheese
- 1/3 cup whole-wheat pastry flour
- 1½ tablespoons coconut oil, melted
- Nonstick cooking spray

DIRECTIONS

1. In a large bowl, lightly whisk the eggs.
2. Whisk in the cottage cheese, flour, and coconut oil just until combined.
3. Heat a large skillet or griddle over medium heat, and lightly coat with the cooking spray.
4. Using a measuring cup, pour 1/3 cup of batter into the skillet for each pancake, boil for 3 minutes and till bubbles appear across the surface of each pancake.
5. Flip over the pancakes and cook for 1 to 2 minutes on the other side, or until golden brown.
6. Serve immediately.
7. Serving tip: Top these pancakes with fresh berries and plain yogurt, unsweetened applesauce, or sugar-free syrup. You can even try them with natural peanut butter and bananas on a general diet.

NUTRITION

Calories: 182   Carbs: 10g   Sodium: 68mg
Total fat: 10g   Fiber: 3g
Protein: 12g   Sugar: 1g

65. Pumpkin Muffins with Walnuts and Zucchini

PREPARATION TIME
10'

COOK TIME
35'

SERVING
4

INGREDIENTS

- Nonstick cooking spray or baking liners
- 2 cups old-fashioned oats
- 1¾ cups whole-wheat pastry flour
- ¼ cup ground flaxseed
- 2 tablespoons baking powder
- 1 teaspoon baking soda
- 1 teaspoon ground cinnamon
- ¼ teaspoon ground nutmeg
- ¼ teaspoon ground ginger
- ¼ teaspoon ground allspice
- 2 cups shredded zucchini
- 1 cup canned pumpkin or fresh pumpkin puree
- 1 cup low-fat milk
- 4 eggs, lightly beaten
- ¼ cup unsweetened applesauce
- 1 teaspoon liquid stevia
- ½ cup chopped walnuts

DIRECTIONS

1. Preheat the oven to 375°F. Prepare two muffin tins by coating the cups with the cooking spray, or use baking liners.
2. In a large bowl, mix together the oats, flour, flaxseed, baking powder, baking soda, cinnamon, nutmeg, ginger, and allspice.
3. In a separate medium bowl mix together the zucchini, pumpkin, milk, eggs, applesauce, and stevia.
4. Add the wet ingredients to the dry and stir to combine. Gently stir in the walnuts.
5. Fill the cups of the muffin tins about half full with the batter.
6. Bake until the muffins are done, when a toothpick inserted in the center comes out clean, about 25 minutes.
7. Let the muffins cool for 5 minutes before removing them from the tins. Place on a baking rack to finish cooling.
8. Wrap leftover muffins in plastic wrap and freeze. Reheat frozen muffins in the microwave for about 20 seconds.

NUTRITION

Calories: 128
Total fat: 5g
Protein: 5g

Carbs: 18g
Fiber: 3g
Sugar: 1g

Sodium: 86mg

66. Hard-Boiled Eggs and Avocado on Toast

PREPARATION TIME
10'

COOK TIME
20'

SERVING
4

INGREDIENTS

- 4 eggs
- 4 slices sprouted whole-wheat bread, such as Angelic Bake House Sprouted Grain
- 1 medium avocado
- 1 teaspoon hot sauce
- Freshly ground black pepper

DIRECTIONS

1. Using a pot, fill it up and rapidly boil over high heat.
2. Carefully add the eggs to the boiling water using a spoon, and set a timer for 10 minutes.
3. Immediately transfer the eggs from the boiling water to a strainer, and run cold water over the eggs to stop the cooking process.
4. Once the eggs are cool enough to handle, peel them and slice lengthwise into fourths.
5. Toast the bread.
6. While the bread toasts, mash the avocado with a fork in a small bowl and mix in the hot sauce.
7. Spread the avocado mash evenly across each toast. Top each toast slice with 4 egg slices and season with the black pepper.

NUTRITION

Calories: 191
Total fat: 10g
Protein: 10g

Carbs: 15g
Fiber: 5g
Sugar: 1g

Sodium: 214mg

67. Yogurt—Based Breakfast Popsicles

PREPARATION TIME
5'

COOK TIME
4 hours

SERVING
6

INGREDIENTS

- ½ cup regular or instant oats
- 1 cup Greek yogurt, plain, non-fat
- 1 cup mixed berries
- ½ cup milk 1% or skim

DIRECTIONS

1. Combine the yogurt and milk.
2. Distribute the milk and yogurt mixture in the Popsicle molds.
3. Add a few berries in all the molds.
4. Distribute the ½ cup oatmeal, evenly among each mound.
5. Leave the popsicles in the freezer for about 5 hours before serving.
6. If the popsicles don't come off easily, keep the mound under a little warm water until they come off loose.

NUTRITION

Calories: 52
Total Fat: 2.9g
Total Carbohydrate: 5.6g

Protein: 1.1g

68. Shrimp Ceviche

PREPARATION TIME
10'

COOK TIME
25'

SERVING
4

INGREDIENTS

- 4 Roma or Italian medium tomatoes, diced or 8 ounces canned tomatoes, diced.
- 1 small red onion, peeled and finely diced or approximately ¾ cup chopped red onion
- 1 bunch of fresh cilantro, stemmed and finely chopped
- 1-pound shrimp medium raw
- 1 cup lime juice or approximately 5 fresh limes, halved
- 2 serrano chili peppers with ribs, seeds removed and minced, if needed.

DIRECTIONS

1. In a large bowl, add the shrimp and lime juice.
2. Cover and let it marinate for 10 to 15 minutes at least or wait until the mixture changes to pink. Do not allow it to marinate for too long or the shrimp will "overcook" and get toughed or rubbery.
3. Combine the onions, tomatoes, cilantro and chili peppers.
4. Slowly stir to combine.
5. Season with salt as required.
6. Serve it when cold.

NUTRITION

Calories: 52
Total Fat: 2.9g
Total Carbohydrate: 5.6g

Protein: 1.1g

69. Chicken Caprese

PREPARATION TIME
15'

COOK TIME
35'

SERVING
4

INGREDIENTS

- 4 thick slices ripe tomato (½-inch)
- 3 tablespoons balsamic vinegar
- 1-pound chicken breasts, boneless and skinless
- 4 1-ounce slices mozzarella cheese
- 1 tablespoon olive oil
- 1 teaspoon dry Italian seasoning or a mixture of garlic powder, dried basil and dried oregano.

- 2 tablespoons thinly sliced fresh basil
- Pepper to season

DIRECTIONS

1. Apply 1 tablespoon of olive oil over the chicken breasts and season as required with salt and pepper.
2. Marinade the chicken with the Italian season and set it aside for 15 minutes.
3. Warm up a skillet or grill over medium to high heat.
4. Keep the chicken on the grill pan and let it cook for about 4–5 minutes on each side, or until it's as cooked as preferred. The cook time alters depending on how thick the chicken breasts are.
5. When the chicken is done, top it with a slice of mozzarella cheese and allow it to cook for another minute.
6. Take it off the heat and keep the chicken breasts on a plate.
7. Garnish the cooked chicken breast with a slice of tomato, evenly sliced basil and season with pepper to taste.
8. Sprinkle with balsamic vinegar or balsamic glaze before serving.

NUTRITION

Calories: 149
Total fat: 4g
Protein: 8g

Carbs: 21g
Fiber: 4g
Sugar: 9g

Sodium: 71 mg

70. Black Bean and Corn Salad

PREPARATION TIME
15'

COOK TIME
35'

SERVING
6

INGREDIENTS

- 2 tablespoons red onion, minced
- ¼ cup balsamic vinegar
- 1 teaspoon lemon juice
- 2 tablespoons olive oil
- 1 cup corn with the whole kernel
- 2 cans of black beans, rinsed and drained (16 ounces can)
- ¼ cup fresh parsley, chopped
- 1 teaspoon garlic, minced
- 1 teaspoon honey
- Salt and pepper for seasoning

DIRECTIONS

1. Combine the fresh corn, red onion, black beans, and fresh parsley in a medium-sized mixing bowl.
2. Transfer the balsamic vinegar, olive oil, lemon juice, honey, garlic, salt and, pepper.
3. Add this mixture to the black beans and corn mixture.
4. Allow the salad to marinate for half an hour before serving.

NUTRITION

Calories: 132
Total fat: 8g
Protein: 10g

Carbohydrates: 6g
Fiber: 1g
Sugar: 3g

Sodium: 255mg.

71. Italian Poached Eggs

PREPARATION TIME
5'

COOK TIME
15'

SERVING
4

INGREDIENTS

- 16 oz. marinara sauce
- 4 shredded basil leaves
- 3–4 roasted red pepper, sliced
- Pepper
- 4 eggs
- Salt

DIRECTIONS

1. Grab a skillet and let it heat up. Add the marinara sauce and the peppers then mix them together and allow them to heat up.
2. Once they are hot, use a spoon to make four wells into the marinara sauce. Now, crack one egg into each of the wells you have made.
3. Sprinkle pepper and salt over each of the eggs.
4. Allow this to cook for about 12 minutes. You can cook the eggs as long as you want until it reaches your desired doneness. You can also place a lid on your skillet so that the eggs cook a bit faster.
5. Remove the skillet from the stove and sprinkle the torn basil over the top. Scoop the eggs out along with a bit of sauce and enjoy.

NUTRITION

Calories: 149   Carbs: 21g   Sodium: 71 mg
Total fat: 4g   Fiber: 4g
Protein: 8g   Sugar: 9g

72. Soft Eggs with Chives and Ricotta

PREPARATION TIME
10'

COOK TIME
30'

SERVING
4

INGREDIENTS

- 2 eggs
- Olive oil
- ½ c milk
- 1 tbsp. chopped chives
- ½ c ricotta

DIRECTIONS

1. Add the eggs and milk to a jar. Place the lid on tightly and shake it until everything is mixed together well.
2. Grab yourself a skillet and place it on the stove. Once it is warm, pour the eggs into the skillet and scramble them. Allow them to cook until they are soft-set. Once soft-set, let it cook and gently stir them once in a while.
3. After the eggs are done, stir the ricotta and the chives. Add the eggs to a plate and drizzle some oil over the top if you would like.

NUTRITION

Calories: 149   Carbs: 21g   Sodium: 71 mg
Total fat: 4g   Fiber: 4g
Protein: 8g   Sugar: 9g

73. Mocha Frappuccino

PREPARATION TIME
10'

COOK TIME
20'

SERVING
4

INGREDIENTS

- ¼ c brewed coffee
- Low-sugar chocolate syrup
- ¼ c unsweetened almond milk
- Low-fat whipped cream
- ½ c 0% fat Greek yogurt
- 1 c ice
- 3–4 drops liquid sweetener
- 1 tbsp. cocoa powder

DIRECTIONS

1. Place the coffee, ice, milk, cocoa, yogurt, and sweetener in a blender and pulse until all of the ingredients come together and it's all smooth.
2. Pour the Frappuccino into a glass and swirl some whipped cream and chocolate syrup over the top.

NUTRITION

Calories: 149	Carbs: 21g	Sodium: 71 mg
Total fat: 4g	Fiber: 4g	
Protein: 8g	Sugar: 9g	

74. Oatmeal Cookie Shake

PREPARATION TIME
10'

COOK TIME
15'

SERVING
3

INGREDIENTS

- Low-fat cream, cinnamon, and nuts—garnish
- 1 c low-fat nut milk
- Ice
- ½ tsp. cinnamon
- ¼ tsp. vanilla
- 1 scoop vanilla whey protein powder
- 1 tbsp. oatmeal

DIRECTIONS

1. Place the protein powder, mice, milk, vanilla, cinnamon, and oatmeal into a strong blender, and pulse a couple of times until all of the ingredients come together.
2. Pour the shake into a glass and top with some cinnamon, cream, and nuts.

NUTRITION

Calories: 232
Total fat: 6g
Protein: 7g

Carbohydrates: 4g
Fiber: 1g
Sugar: 2g

Sodium: 155mg.

75. Bun less Breakfast Sandwich

PREPARATION TIME
10'

COOK TIME
5'

SERVING
2

INGREDIENTS

- ¼ c shredded cheddar cheese
- 2 eggs
- 2 tbsp. water
- ½ avocado, mashed
- 2 sliced cooked bacon

DIRECTIONS

1. Place two canning jar lids into a skillet and spray with cooking spray. Let everything warm up. Crack one egg in each lid and whisk the egg gently with a fork to break the yolks.
2. Pour a small amount of water into the pan and put the lid on the skillet. Allow to cook and steam the eggs. Cook for three minutes. Take off the lid and put cheese on just one of the eggs. Allow cheese to melt for about one minute.
3. Put the egg without the cheese on a plate. Add avocado and then the bacon on top. Put the other egg on top with the cheesy side down. Enjoy.

NUTRITION

Calories: 234   Carbohydrates: 7g   Sodium: 264 mg.
Total fat: 9g   Fiber: 2g
Protein: 11g   Sugar: 3g

76. Ham and Egg Roll-Ups

PREPARATION TIME
10'

COOK TIME
15'

SERVING
6

INGREDIENTS

- 2 tsp. garlic powder
- 1 c baby spinach
- 1 c chopped tomatoes
- 10 eggs
- Pepper
- 2 tbsp. butter
- Salt
- 1 ½ c shredded cheddar cheese
- 20 ham slices

DIRECTIONS

1. Turn oven to broil. Crack all the eggs into a bowl and beat them together. Add the garlic powder, pepper, and salt. Mix well.
2. Warm a skillet on the stovetop. Add the butter and allow it to melt. Add the eggs and scramble until they are done. Mix the cheese, stirring until it melts. Fold in the spinach and tomatoes.
3. Put two pieces of ham on a cutting board. Add a spoonful of eggs then roll up. Repeat this process until all ham and eggs are used.
4. Place the roll-ups on a baking sheet and broil for about five minutes.

NUTRITION

Calories: 149   Carbs: 21g   Sodium: 71 mg
Total fat: 4g   Fiber: 4g
Protein: 8g   Sugar: 9g

77. Chocolate Porridge

PREPARATION TIME
10'

COOK TIME
30'

SERVING
4

INGREDIENTS

- Chopped nuts, fruits, or seeds of choice
- 4 tbsp. porridge oats
- 1 c skim milk
- Sugar-free syrup
- 1 square dark unsweetened chocolate
- 1 tbsp. cocoa powder

DIRECTIONS

1. Place the chocolate, cocoa powder, oats, and milk in a microwavable bowl.
2. Cook for two minutes. Give everything a good stir and cook for an additional 15 to 20 seconds.
3. Put in a serving bowl and add desired toppings. Enjoy.

NUTRITION

Calories: 149
Total fat: 4g
Protein: 8g

Carbs: 21g
Fiber: 4g
Sugar: 9g

Sodium: 71 mg

78. Flour-Less Pancakes

PREPARATION TIME
15'

COOK TIME
20'

SERVING
2

INGREDIENTS

- Milk to mix
- 1 egg
- Low-fat cooking spray
- 1 c rolled oats
- 1 banana

DIRECTIONS

1. Place the banana, egg, and oats into a food processor. Process until smooth. Add a small amount of milk and blend again. Add the milk until the mixture has reached a runny consistency. Three tablespoons should be the maximum amount you use.
2. Allow sitting for about 15 minutes. This lets the mixture thicken slightly.
3. Spray a small amount of cooking spray into a skillet. Let it warm up. Add a spoonful of the batter to form a small pancake. Put as many as your pan will allow. Just make sure you have room to flip each. Allow the first side to cook for about a minute until bubbles begin to form on the surface. Flip and cook until browned. Remove from the skillet onto a plate and keep warm while you continue to cook the remaining batter.
4. Serve warm with fruit, yogurt, sugar-free syrup, a dusting of powdered sugar, or a drizzle of lemon. You might prefer them plain. Either way, enjoy.

NUTRITION

Calories: 149
Total fat: 4g
Protein: 8g

Carbs: 21g
Fiber: 4g
Sugar: 9g

Sodium: 71 mg

79. Cheesy Spiced Pancakes

PREPARATION TIME
15'

COOK TIME
20'

SERVING
3

INGREDIENTS

- Pancakes:
- 1 tbsp. artificial sweetener
- 1 tsp. mixed spice, ground
- Low-fat cooking spray
- 8 oz. spreadable goat cheese
- Pinch salt
- 3 eggs, separated
- ½ c all-purpose flour
- Optional Adult Toppings:

- Sweetener
- 1 measure Brandy
- 4 tangerines, peeled
- 2 oz. cranberries

DIRECTIONS

1. To make the pancakes: Combine the egg yolks, cheese, and mixed spice. Add the salt and flour and mix well.
2. Beat the egg whites until they are stiff peaks and whisk in sweetener. Fold this into the cheese mixture.
3. If using the optional topping, place sweetener and tangerines into a pot. Stir occasionally until tangerines begin to release some juices and begin to look a bit syrupy. Add the Brandy and cranberries. Let this cook for few minutes. Keep warm until ready to use.
4. Spray the skillet with cooking spray. Allow to warm up. Add three large spoonfuls of batter into the pan. Cook for about two minutes until bubbles form on top. Flip and cook until the other side is browned. Remove from the pan and keep warm. Continue until all batter has been used. You should get 12 pancakes from this batter.
5. Divide among four plates and spoon the topping. Enjoy.

NUTRITION

Calories: 149
Total fat: 4g
Protein: 8g

Carbs: 21g
Fiber: 4g
Sugar: 9g

Sodium: 71 mg

80. Egg Muffin

PREPARATION TIME
10'

COOK TIME
20'

SERVING
4

INGREDIENTS

- ¼ tsp. salt
- 12 slices turkey bacon
- ¼ tsp. Italian seasoning
- 6 large eggs
- ¼ tsp. pepper
- ¾ c shredded low-fat shredded cheese of choice
- ½ c 1% milk

DIRECTIONS

1. Spray cooking spray into muffin pan. Your oven needs to be warmed to 350°F.
2. Place three slices of bacon on the bottom of each muffin cup.
3. Mix all remaining ingredients together until well combined. Reserve ¼ cup of shredded cheese. Put ¼ cup of this mixture into every muffin cup. Add a bit more cheese on top.
4. Bake for about 25 minutes. The eggs should be set.

NUTRITION

Calories: 149   Carbs: 21g   Sodium: 71 mg
Total fat: 4g   Fiber: 4g
Protein: 8g   Sugar: 9g

81. Cottage Cheese Pancakes

PREPARATION TIME
10'

COOK TIME
15'

SERVING
4

INGREDIENTS

- 1/3 c all-purpose flour
- ½ tbsp. canola oil
- ½ tsp. baking soda
- 3 eggs, lightly beaten
- 1 c low-fat cottage cheese

DIRECTIONS

1. Sift the baking soda and flour in a small bowl.
2. Mix the remaining ingredients together.
3. Mix the flour into the wet ingredients and stir to incorporate.
4. Spray cooking spray into a skillet and warm. When warmed, place one-third cup of the batter into the pan and cook until you see bubbles. Flip and cook until the other side is browned.
5. Serve warm with sugar-free syrup. Enjoy.

NUTRITION

Calories: 149
Total fat: 4g
Protein: 8g

Carbs: 21g
Fiber: 4g
Sugar: 9g

Sodium: 71 mg

CHAPTER 7
Lunch

82. Sheet Pan Zucchini Parmesan

PREPARATION TIME
10'

COOK TIME
25'

SERVING
6

INGREDIENTS

- 1 cup panko
- 1/3 cup freshly grated parmesan cheese
- Kosher salt and freshly ground black pepper, to taste
- 2 zucchinis, thinly sliced to 1/4-inch thick rounds
- 1/3 cup all-purpose flour
- 2 large eggs, beaten
- ½ cup marinara sauce
- ½ cup mozzarella pearls, drained
- 2 tablespoons chopped fresh parsley leaves

DIRECTIONS

1. Preheat broiler to 400°F. Daintily oil a preparing sheet or coat with a nonstick shower.
2. In an enormous bowl, consolidate panko and parmesan; season with salt and pepper, to taste. Put in a safe spot.
3. Working in clumps, dig zucchini adjusts in flour and dunk into eggs. At that point, dig in panko blend and squeezing to cover.
4. Spot zucchini in a solitary layer onto the readied heating sheet. Spot into stove and heat until delicate and brilliant dark-colored, around 18 to 20 minutes.
5. Top with marinara and mozzarella.
6. At that point cook for 2 to 3minutes, or until the cheddar has dissolved.
7. Servings quickly, embellished with parsley, whenever wanted.

NUTRITION

Calories: 217
Protein: 11g
Carbs: 21g

Fat: 12g
Protein:

83. Grilled Fig and Peach Arugula Salad with Ricotta Salute and a Black Pepper Vinaigrette Print

PREPARATION TIME
10'

COOK TIME
20'

SERVING
2

INGREDIENTS

Dressing:
- 3 tablespoons good-quality olive oil
- 1 teaspoon good balsamic vinegar
- ½ lemon from juice
- Salt
- 6 to 7 turns freshly ground pepper

Salad:
- 4 figs, halved
- 1 teaspoon dark brown sugar

- Salt
- Olive oil
- Few handfuls of arugulas, 2 ounces, cleaned and dried
- 1 yellow peach, sliced
- 3 to 4 pistachios, chopped
- 2 slices prosciutto
- ¼ cup of Ricotta Salata

DIRECTIONS

1. In a little bowl, including the olive oil, balsamic vinegar, lemon juice, squeeze of salt and naturally ground pepper; blend until altogether joined. Do a trial and include more salt, in the event that you like. Put in a safe spot.
2. Sprinkle the figs with the dim dark-colored sugar and a touch of salt. Warmth a barbecue or flame broil skillet. Whenever hot, brush with olive oil. Spot the figs on the hot flame broil, face down and cook for 1-minutes, until barbecue imprints show up. Expel and put in a safe spot.
3. To a huge blending bowl, include the arugula. Sprinkle the leaves with salt. Include half of the dressing and delicately prepare the serving of mixed greens.
4. Move the lettuce to your serving plate. Add the peaches to the blending bowl and hurl with a touch of dressing.
5. Move the peaches and figs to the serving plate, masterminding any way you like. Top with a sprinkling of pistachios, a couple of torn bits of prosciutto and slight cuts of Ricotta Salata.

NUTRITION

Calories: 3
Carbs: 26g
Fat: 24g

Protein: 10g

84. Lean Spring Stew

PREPARATION TIME
15'

COOK TIME
1h 15'

SERVING
4

INGREDIENTS

- 1 lb. fire-roasted tomatoes, diced
- 4 boneless, skinless chicken thighs
- 1 tbsp. dried basil
- 8 oz. chicken stock
- Salt & pepper to taste
- 4 oz. tomato paste
- 3 chopped celery stalks
- 3 chopped carrots
- 2 chili peppers, finely chopped
- 2 tbsp. olive oil
- 1 finely chopped onion
- 2 garlic cloves, crushed
- ½ container mushrooms sour cream

DIRECTIONS

1. Heat up the olive oil over medium-high temperature. Add the celery, onions and carrots and stir-fry for 5 to minutes.
2. Transfer to a deep pot and add tomato paste, basil, garlic, mushrooms and seasoning. Keep stirring the vegetables until they are completely covered by tomato sauce. At the same time, cut the chicken into small cubes to make it easier to eat.
3. Put the chicken in a deep pot, pour the chicken stock over it and throw in the tomatoes.
4. Stir the chicken in to ensure the ingredients and vegetables are properly mixed with it. Turn the heat to low and cook for about an hour. The vegetables and chicken should be cooked through before you turn the heat off. Top with sour cream and serve!

NUTRITION

Net carbs 19 g
Fiber 3 g
Fats 11.9 g

Fats: 3 g
Calories 277

85. Yummy Chicken Bites

PREPARATION TIME
10'

COOK TIME
10'

SERVING
2

INGREDIENTS

- 1 lb. chicken breasts, skinless, boneless and cut into cubes
- 2 tbsp. fresh lemon juice
- 1 tbsp. fresh oregano, chopped
- 2 tbsp. olive oil
- 1/8 tsp cayenne pepper
- Pepper
- Salt

DIRECTIONS

1. Place chicken in a bowl.
2. Add reaming ingredients over chicken and mix well.
3. Place chicken in the refrigerator for 1 hour.
4. Heat grill over medium heat.
5. Spray grill with cooking spray.
6. Thread marinated chicken onto skewers.
7. Arrange skewers on the grill and grill until the chicken is cooked.
8. Serve and enjoy.

NUTRITION

Calories 560
Fat 31 g
Carbohydrates 1.8 g

Sugar 0.4 g
Protein 66 g
Cholesterol 200 mg

86. Shrimp Scampi

PREPARATION TIME
5'

COOK TIME
10'

SERVING
4

INGREDIENTS

- 1 lb. Shrimp
- 1/4 tsp red pepper flakes
- 1 tbsp. fresh lemon juice
- 1/4 cup butter
- 1/2 cup chicken broth
- 2 garlic cloves, minced
- 1 shallot, sliced
- 3 tbsp. olive oil
- 3 tbsp. parsley, chopped
- Pepper
- Salt

DIRECTIONS

1. Heat oil in a pan over medium heat.
2. Add garlic and shallots and cook for 3 minutes.
3. Add broth, lemon juice, and butter and cook for 5 minutes.
4. Add red pepper flakes, parsley, pepper, and salt. Stir.
5. Add shrimp and cook for 3 minutes.
6. Serve and enjoy.

NUTRITION

Calories 336;
Fat 24 g;
Carbohydrates 3 g;

Sugar 0.2 g;
Protein 26 g;
Cholesterol 269 mg

87. Zucchini Frittata

PREPARATION TIME
10'

COOK TIME
10'

SERVING
4

INGREDIENTS

- 2 teaspoons butter (divided)
- 1 cup shredded zucchini
- Salt and freshly ground black pepper, to taste
- 4 eggs (lightly beaten)
- 2 tablespoons skim milk
- 1/4 teaspoon garlic salt
- 1/4 teaspoon onion powder
- 2 tablespoons shredded mild cheddar cheese

DIRECTIONS

1. In a medium nonstick skillet over medium heat, melt teaspoon butter and sauté zucchini until softened and lightly browned, 4 to 5 minutes, stirring frequently.
2. Drain zucchini if necessary and season to taste with salt and pepper. Beat eggs with milk, garlic salt, onion powder and zucchini until combined. Melt remaining 1 teaspoon butter in skillet, add egg mixture and cook until partially set. Lift edges of cooked egg with a spatula, let uncooked egg run underneath and continue until top of frittata is set, about 4 minutes.
3. Carefully flip frittata and let cook until lightly browned, to 4 minutes. Remove skillet from heat, sprinkle cheese over frittata and let stand until cheese is melted.
4. Cut frittata in half and serve immediately. Enjoy!

NUTRITION

Calories: 20
Total Fat: 15g
Saturated Fat: 7g

Protein: 14g
Carbs: 4g
Fiber: 1Ùg

Sugar: 3g

88. Salmon Patties

PREPARATION TIME
10'

COOK TIME
10'

SERVING
3

INGREDIENTS

- 14.5 oz. can salmon
- 4 tbsp. butter
- 1 avocado, diced
- 2 eggs, lightly beaten
- 1/2 cup almond flour
- 1/2 onion, minced
- Pepper
- Salt

DIRECTIONS

1. Add all ingredients except butter in a large mixing bowl and mix until well combined.
2. Make six patties from the mixture. Set aside.
3. Melt butter in a pan over medium heat.
4. Place patties on pan and cook for 5 minutes on each side.
5. Serve and enjoy.

NUTRITION

Calories 9
Fat 49 g
Carbohydrates 11 g

Sugar 2 g
Protein 36 g
Cholesterol 225 mg

89. Apple Cinnamon Oatmeal

PREPARATION TIME
10'

COOK TIME
10'

SERVING
1

INGREDIENTS

- 1/2 cup skim milk
- 1/3 cup water
- 1 apple (peeled, cored, diced)
- Dash salt
- 1/2 cup old fashioned oats
- 1/4 teaspoon cinnamon
- 1/4 teaspoon vanilla

DIRECTIONS

1. Mix milk, water, apple and salt in a small saucepan and heat to a simmer, stirring occasionally (do not boil).
2. Add oats and cinnamon to the saucepan and simmer, uncovered, for about 5 minutes, stirring occasionally.
3. Stir vanilla into oatmeal and serve immediately. Enjoy!

NUTRITION

Calories: 18
Total Fat: 2g
Saturated Fat: 0g

Protein: 7g
Carbs: 36g
Fiber: 4g

Sugar: 19g

90. Stuff Cheese Pork Chops

PREPARATION TIME
10'

COOK TIME
25'

SERVING
4

INGREDIENTS

- 4 pork chops, boneless and thick cut
- 2 tbsp. olives, chopped
- 2 tbsp. sun-dried tomatoes, chopped
- ½ cup feta cheese, crumbled
- 2 garlic cloves, minced
- 2 tbsp. fresh parsley, chopped

DIRECTIONS

1. Preheat the oven to 375°F.
2. In a bowl, mix together feta cheese, garlic, parsley, olives, and sun-dried tomatoes.
3. Stuff feta cheese mixture in the pork chops. Season with pepper and salt.
4. Bake for 35 minutes.
5. Serve and enjoy.

NUTRITION

Calories: 31
Fat: 25 g
Carbohydrates: 2 g

Sugar: 1 g
Protein: 21 g
Cholesterol: 75 mg

91. Italian Pork Chops

PREPARATION TIME
10'

COOK TIME
30'

SERVING
4

INGREDIENTS

- 4 pork loin chops, boneless
- 2 garlic cloves, minced
- 1 tsp Italian seasoning
- 1 tbsp. fresh rosemary, chopped
- 1/4 tsp black pepper
- 1/2 tsp kosher salt

DIRECTIONS

1. Season pork chops with pepper and salt.
2. In a small bowl, mix together garlic, Italian seasoning, and rosemary.
3. Rub pork chops with garlic and rosemary mixture.
4. Place pork chops on a baking tray and roast in the oven at 375 F for 10 minutes.
5. Turn temperature to 300 F and roast for 25 minutes more.
6. Serve and enjoy.

NUTRITION

Calories: 261
Fat: 19 g
Carbohydrates: 2 g

Sugar: 0 g
Protein: 18 g
Cholesterol: 68 mg

Fiber: 0.4 g
Net carbs: 1 g

92. Sunshine Wrap

PREPARATION TIME
10'

COOK TIME
30'

SERVING
2

INGREDIENTS

- 8 oz. Grilled chicken breast
- ½ c. Diced celery
- 2/3 c. Mandarin oranges
- ¼ c. Minced onion
- 2 tbsps. Mayonnaise
- 1 tsp. Soy sauce
- ¼ tsp. Garlic powder
- ¼ tsp. Black pepper
- 1 whole wheat tortilla
- 4 lettuce leaves

DIRECTIONS

1. Combine all ingredients, except tortilla and lettuce, in a large bowl and toss to evenly coat.
2. Lay tortillas on a flat surface and cut them into quarters.
3. Top each quarter with a lettuce leaf and spoon chicken mixture into the middle of each.
4. Roll each tortilla into a cone and seal by slightly wetting the edge with water. Enjoy!

NUTRITION

Calories: 280.8
Fat: 21.1g
Carbs: 3g

Protein: 19g

93. Taco Omelet

PREPARATION TIME
10'

COOK TIME
10'

SERVING
1

INGREDIENTS

- 2 eggs (lightly beaten)
- 2 tablespoons skim milk
- 1/4 teaspoon chili powder
- 1/4 teaspoon garlic powder
- 1/4 teaspoon onion powder
- Salt and freshly ground black pepper, to taste
- 1 teaspoon vegetable oil
- 1 tablespoon guacamole
- 1 tablespoon sour cream
- 1 tablespoon salsa
- 2 tablespoons shredded Colby Jack cheese

DIRECTIONS

1. In a medium bowl, whisk eggs, milk, chili powder, garlic powder and onion powder and season to taste with salt and pepper.
2. Heat oil in a medium nonstick skillet over medium heat. Pour egg mixture into skillet and swirl to coat evenly. Cover skillet and let eggs cook until set on top, about 4 minutes.
3. With a large spatula, carefully flip the omelet. Season omelet to taste with salt and pepper and let cook until lightly browned on the bottom, about minutes more.
4. Slide omelet onto a plate. Spread guacamole, sour cream and salsa all over one side of the omelet and sprinkle with cheese. Fold omelet in half over filling and serve immediately. Enjoy

NUTRITION

Calories: 290   Protein: 17g   Sugar: 3g
Total Fat: 22g   Carbs: 6g
Saturated Fat: 10g   Fiber: 1g

94. Sheet Pan Spicy Tofu and Green Beans

PREPARATION TIME
10'

COOK TIME
30'

SERVING
4

INGREDIENTS

- Spicy marinade:
- 1 teaspoon minced garlic
- ¼ cup sliced scallions
- 2 teaspoons sesame seeds, plus more for garnish
- 3 tablespoons soy sauce
- 1 tablespoon sesame oil
- 1 teaspoon red pepper flakes
- ½ teaspoon maple syrup

- 2 tablespoons of rice wine vinegar
- 16 ounces firm tofu, drained and pressed
- 1 pound green beans, trimmed
- 2 teaspoons olive oil, for oiling the pan
- Salt/pepper

DIRECTIONS

1. Preheat the broiler to 400°F.
2. Flush and channel your tofu, at that point press utilizing a tofu press or envelop with paper towels and spot overwhelming books or dish on top. Let channel for in any event 10 to 15 minutes, this will enable the marinade to be assimilated.
3. Whisk together the elements for the zesty sauce.
4. Cut the tofu into triangles and spot in a solitary layer on an oiled preparing sheet. Shower with the hot sauce at that point prepares for 12 minutes.
5. Flip tofu and sprinkle with more sauce. Add the green beans to the opposite side of the container in a solitary layer, as would be prudent. Shower with residual sauce and sprinkle with salt and pepper.
6. Return back to the stove and heat until tofu is caramelized and somewhat fresh, around 12–15 minutes.
7. Sprinkle with residual sesame seeds, whenever wanted, and serve.

NUTRITION

Calories: 21
Carbs: 20g
Fat: 11g

Protein: 12g

95. Skillet Chicken Thighs with Potato, Apple, and Spinach

PREPARATION TIME
10'

COOK TIME
20'

SERVING
1

INGREDIENTS

- 1 small chicken thigh
- Salt
- Pepper
- 1 teaspoon canola oil
- 1 medium russet potato, cut into ½ inch cubes.
- 1 small Fuji apple, cored and cut into 6 wedges.
- 1 teaspoon fresh sage, chopped.
- 1 cup packed baby spinach

DIRECTIONS

1. Warm broiler to 400°F.
2. Season bird generously with salt and pepper.
3. In an extensive broiler-secure skillet over medium warmth, warm up the oil. Include bird, skin side down, and prepare dinner till pores and skin crisps marginally and a few fats are rendered round minutes. Include potato, apple, and sage. Toss to cowl and arrange potato and apple around the skillet, making sure the chicken is skin-side down.
4. Move skillet to broiler and dish for 15 minutes. Flip chicken, at that factor, broil 10 minutes extra, till potatoes and apples are delicate and chicken is cooked thru with no red within the middle.
5. Return skillet to stovetop over medium-low heat. Take off the chicken, consist of spinach and hurl with potatoes and apples to shrivel.
6. Top vegetable mixture with chook to serve.

NUTRITION

Calories: 514
Fat: 22g
Carbs: 59g

Sugar: 23g
Protein: 21g

96. Cherry Tomatoes Tilapia Salad

PREPARATION TIME
10'

COOK TIME
25'

SERVING
3

INGREDIENTS

- 1 c. Mixed greens
- 1 c. Cherry tomatoes
- 1/3 c. Diced red onion.
- 1 medium avocado
- 3 tortilla-crusted tilapia fillet.

DIRECTIONS

1. Spray tilapia fillet with a little bit of cooking spray. Put fillets in the air fryer basket. Cook for 25 minutes at about 390°F.
2. Transfer the fillet to a bowl. Toss with tomatoes, greens and red onion. Add the lime dressing and mix again.
3. Serve and enjoy!

NUTRITION

Calories: 271
Fat: 8g
Carbs: 10.1g

Protein: 18.5g

97. Apple Cider Glazed Chicken Breast with Carrots

PREPARATION TIME
10'

COOK TIME
6h 45'

SERVING
2

INGREDIENTS

- 2 boneless skin-on chicken breasts
- 2 cups apple cider
- 4 whole peppercorns
- 2 small bunches of fresh sage
- ½ teaspoon salt

- 2 tablespoons olive oil
- Salt and pepper, to taste
- 4 carrots, peeled and sliced.
- 1 tablespoon butter

DIRECTIONS

1. To start with, in all probability, your boneless skin-on chicken bosom still has the tenderloin connected. Expel (it's the additional piece that resembles a chicken strip). This helps the chicken cook quicker. I solidify the tenderloins for soup or make chicken strips with them.
2. In an enormous dish or bowl, include the chicken, apple juice, peppercorns, sage (torn and hacked first), and ½ teaspoon of salt. Let marinate shrouded in the cooler for at least 4hrs.
3. Following 4hrs, expel the chicken and pat the chicken dry. Warm the oil in a huge skillet. At the point when the oil is hot, sprinkle the chicken with additional salt and pepper and spot its skin-side down in the container. Cook on both sides until brilliant darker.
4. In the meantime, strip and bones the carrots. Spot them in a microwave-safe bowl, spread with saran wrap and microwave for 1 moment.
5. Take the flavors out from the apple juice, and after that pour it over the chicken once the two sides are brilliant dark colored. Change the warmth so the apple juice goes to a stew and cook until the chicken registers 160°F on a thermometer. Evacuate the chicken and put it aside when done.
6. When the chicken is done, turn from warmth to high and lessen the apple juice to a thick coat. Include the carrots and sauté for 3 to 4 minutes, until fresh delicate. Include the spread before expelling them from the dish. Mix to cover the carrots in the coating and margarine. Utilize any additional coating from the dish to brush on the chicken and serve the chicken with the carrots.

NUTRITION

Calories: 328
Fat: 20g
Carbs: 39g

Sugar: 2.
Protein: 2g

98. Onion Paprika Pork Tenderloin

PREPARATION TIME
10'

COOK TIME
30'

SERVING
6

INGREDIENTS

- 2 lbs. Pork tenderloin
- For rub:
- 1 1/2 tbsp. smoked paprika
- 1 tbsp. garlic powder
- 1 1/2 tbsp. onion powder
- ½ tbsp. salt

DIRECTIONS

1. Preheat the oven to 425°F.
2. In a small bowl, mix together all rub ingredients and rub over pork tenderloin.
3. Spray pan with cooking spray and heat over medium-high heat.
4. Sear pork on all sides until lightly golden brown.
5. Place pan into the oven and roast for about 4hrs.
6. Sliced and serve.

NUTRITION

Calories: 225
Fat: 5 g
Carbohydrates: 2 g

Sugar: 1 g
Protein: 41 g
Cholesterol: 45 mg

99. Rosemary Garlic Pork Chops

PREPARATION TIME
10'

COOK TIME
35'

SERVING
4

INGREDIENTS

- 4 pork chops, boneless
- ¼ tsp onion powder
- 2 garlic cloves, minced.
- 1 tsp dried rosemary, crushed.
- ¼ tsp pepper
- ¼ tsp sea salt

DIRECTIONS

1. Preheat the oven to 425°F.
2. Season pork chops with onion powder, pepper and salt.
3. Mix together rosemary and garlic and rub over pork chops.
4. Place pork chops on baking tray and roast for 10 minutes.
5. Set temperature 3 f and roast for 25 minutes more.
6. Serve and enjoy.

NUTRITION

Calories: 260
Fat: 20 g
Carbohydrates: 1 g

Sugar: 0 g
Protein: 19 g
Cholesterol: mg

100. Skinny Chicken Pesto Bake

PREPARATION TIME
10'

COOK TIME
35'

SERVING
4

INGREDIENTS

- 160 oz. Skinless chicken
- 1 tsps. Basil
- 1 sliced tomato
- 6 tbsps. Shredded mozzarella cheese
- 2 tsps. Grated parmesan cheese

DIRECTIONS

1. Cut chicken into thin strips.
2. Set oven to 400°F. Prepare a baking sheet by lining it with parchment paper.
3. Lay chicken strips on prepared baking sheet. Top with pesto and brush evenly over chicken pieces.
4. Set to bake until chicken is fully cooked (about 15 minutes).
5. Garnish with parmesan cheese, mozzarella, and tomatoes.
6. Set to continue baking until cheese melts (about 5 minutes).

NUTRITION

Calories: 205
Fat: 8.5g
Carbs: 2.5g

Protein: 30g

101. Cold Tomato Couscous

PREPARATION TIME
10'

COOK TIME
10'

SERVING
4

INGREDIENTS

- 5 oz. couscous
- 3 tbsp. tomato sauce
- 3 tbsp. lemon juice
- 1 small-sized onion, chopped.
- 1 cup vegetable stock
- ½ small-sized cucumber, sliced.
- ½ small-sized carrot, sliced.
- ¼ tsp salt3 tbsp. olive oil
- ½ cup fresh parsley, chopped.

DIRECTIONS

1. First, pour the couscous into a large bowl. Boil the vegetable broth and slightly add in the couscous while stirring constantly. Leave it for about 5 minutes until the couscous absorbs the liquid. Cover with a lid and set aside. Stir from time to time to speed up the soaking process and break the lumps with a spoon.
2. Meanwhile, preheat the olive oil in a frying pan, and add the tomato sauce. Add chopped onion and stir until translucent. Set aside and let it cool for a few minutes.
3. Add the oily tomato sauce to the couscous and stir well. Now add lemon juice, chopped parsley, and salt to the mixture and give it a final stir.
4. Serve with sliced cucumber, carrot, and parsley.

NUTRITION

Net carbs: 32.8 g
Fiber: 3.2 g
Fats: 11 g

Fats: 6 g
Calories: 249

102. Fresh Shrimp Spring Rolls

PREPARATION TIME
10'

COOK TIME
20'

SERVING
12

INGREDIENTS

- 12 sheets rice paper
- 12 bib lettuce
- 12 basil leaves.
- ¾ c. cilantro
- 1 c. shredded carrots
- ½ sliced cucumber.
- 20 oz. cooked shrimp

DIRECTIONS

1. Add all vegetables and shrimp to separate bowls.
2. Set a damp paper towel tower flat on the work surface.
3. Quickly wet a sheet of rice paper under warm water and lay it on a paper towel.
4. Top with 1 of each vegetable and 4 pieces of shrimp, then roll in rice paper into a burrito-like roll.
5. Repeat until all vegetables and shrimp have been used up. Serve and enjoy.

NUTRITION

Calories: 67
Fat: 2.9g
Carbs: 7.4g

Protein: 2.6g

103. Chicken Breast Tortilla

PREPARATION TIME
10'

COOK TIME
30'

SERVING
2

INGREDIENTS

- 8 oz. grilled chicken breast
- ½ c. diced celery
- 2/3 c. mandarin oranges
- ¼ c. minced onion
- 2 tbsps. mayonnaise
- 1 tsp. soy sauce
- ¼ tsp. garlic powder
- ¼ tsp. black pepper
- 1 whole wheat tortilla

- 4 lettuce leaves

DIRECTIONS

1. Combine all ingredients, except tortilla and lettuce, in a large bowl and toss to evenly coat.
2. Lay tortillas on a flat surface and cut them into quarters.
3. Top each quarter with a lettuce leaf and spoon chicken mixture into the middle of each.
4. Roll each tortilla into a cone and seal by slightly wetting the edge with water. Enjoy!

NUTRITION

Calories: 280.8
Fat: 21.1g
Carbs: 3g

Protein: 19g

104. Sweet Roasted Beet & Arugula Tortilla Pizza V

PREPARATION TIME
10'

COOK TIME
25'

SERVING
6

INGREDIENTS

- 2 chopped Beets
- 6 Corn Tortillas
- 1 c. Arugula
- ½ c. Goat cheese
- 1 c. Blackberries
- 2 tbsps. Honey
- 2 tbsps. Balsamic vinegar

DIRECTIONS

1. Preheat oven to 350°F. Lay tortillas on a flat surface.
2. Top with beets, berries and goat cheese. Combine balsamic vinegar and honey together in a small bowl and whisk to combine.
3. Drizzle the mixture over pizza and bake for about 10 minutes, or until cheese has melted slightly and the tortilla is crisp.
4. Garnish with arugula and serve.

NUTRITION

Calories: 286
Fat: 40g
Carbs: 42g

Protein: 15g

105. Southwestern Black Bean Cakes with Guacamole

PREPARATION TIME
10'

COOK TIME
25'

SERVING
4

INGREDIENTS

- 1 c. whole wheat bread crumbs
- 3 tbsps. chopped cilantro
- 2 garlic cloves
- 15 oz. black beans
- 7 oz. chipotle peppers in adobo sauce
- 1 tsp. ground cumin
- 1 large egg
- ½ diced avocado
- 1 tbsp. lime juice
- 1 tomato plum

DIRECTIONS

1. Drain beans and add all ingredients, except avocado, lime juice and eggs, to a food processor and run until the mixture begins to pull away from the sides.
2. Transfer to a large bowl and add egg, then mix well.
3. Form into 4 even patties and cook on a preheated, greased grill over medium heat for about 10 minutes, flipping halfway through.
4. Add avocado and lime juice in a small bowl, then stir and mash together using a fork.
5. Season to taste then serve with bean cakes.

NUTRITION

Calories: 178
Fat: 7g
Carbs: 25g

Protein: 11g

106. Veggie Quesadillas with Cilantro Yogurt Dip

PREPARATION TIME
10'

COOK TIME
25'

SERVING
3

INGREDIENTS

- 1 c. black beans
- 2 tbsp chopped cilantro.
- ½ chopped bell pepper.
- ½ c. corn kernels
- 1 c. shredded cheese
- 6 corn tortillas
- 1 shredded carrot

DIRECTIONS

1. Set skillet to preheat on low heat. Lay 3 tortillas on a flat surface.
2. Top evenly with peppers, carrots, cilantro, beans, corn and cheese over the tortillas, covering each with another tortilla, maximum.
3. Add quesadilla to a preheated skillet. Cook until the cheese melts and the tortilla gets a nice golden brown (about 2 min).
4. Flip quesadilla and cook for about a minute or until golden.
5. Mix well. Slice each quesadilla into 4 even wedges and serve with dip. Enjoy!

NUTRITION

Calories: 344
Fat: 8g
Carbs: 46g

Protein: 27g

107. Mayo-less Tuna Salad

PREPARATION TIME
10'

COOK TIME
5'

SERVING
2

INGREDIENTS

- 5 oz. tuna
- 1 tbsp. olive oil
- 1 tbsp. red wine vinegar
- ¼ c. chopped green onion.
- 2 c. arugula
- 1 c. cooked pasta
- 1 tbsp. parmesan cheese
- Black pepper

DIRECTIONS

1. Combine all ingredients into a medium bowl. Split mixture between two plates. Serve, and enjoy.

NUTRITION

Calories: 213.2   Protein: 22.7g
Fat: 6.2g
Carbs: 20.3g

108. Southwest Style Zucchini Rice Bowl

PREPARATION TIME
10'

COOK TIME
12'

SERVING
2

INGREDIENTS

- 1 tbsp. vegetable oil
- 1 c. chopped vegetables.
- 1 c. chopped chicken breast.
- 1 c. cooked zucchini rice
- 4 tbsps. salsa
- 2 tbsps. shredded cheddar cheese
- 2 tbsps. sour cream

DIRECTIONS

1. Set a skillet with oil to heat up over medium heat.
2. Add chopped vegetables and allow to cook, stirring until vegetables become fork tender.
3. Add chicken and zucchini rice. Cook while stirring until fully heated through.
4. Split between 2 serving bowls and garnish with remaining ingredients. Serve and enjoy!

NUTRITION

Calories: 168
Fat: 8.2g
Carbs: 18g

Protein: 5.5g

109. Pesto & Mozzarella Stuffed Portobello Mushroom Caps

PREPARATION TIME
10'

COOK TIME
30'

SERVING
2

INGREDIENTS

- 2 portobello mushrooms
- 1 diced Roma tomato
- 2 tbsps. pesto
- ¼ c. shredded mozzarella cheese

DIRECTIONS

1. Spoon pesto evenly into mushroom caps, then top with remaining ingredients.
2. Bake at 400°F for about 15 minutes. Enjoy!

NUTRITION

Calories: 112   Protein: 10.5g
Fat: 5.4g
Carbs: 7.5g

110. Tandoori Chicken

PREPARATION TIME
10'

COOK TIME
35'

SERVING
6

INGREDIENTS

- 1 c. plain yogurt
- ½ c, lemon juice
- 5 crushed garlic cloves
- 2 tbsps. paprika
- 1 tsp. yellow curry powder
- 1 tsp. ground ginger
- 6 skinless chicken breasts
- 6 skewers

DIRECTIONS

1. Set oven to 400°F. In a blender, combine red pepper flakes, ginger, curry, paprika, garlic, lemon juice and yogurt, then process into a smooth paste.
2. Add chicken strips evenly onto skewers. Add chicken to a shallow casserole dish then cover with ½ of yogurt mixture.
3. Tightly seal and rest in the refrigerator for about 15 minutes.
4. Lightly grease a baking tray, then transfer chicken skewers onto it, and top with the remaining yogurt mixture.
5. Set to bake until the chicken is fully cooked. Serve and enjoy.

NUTRITION

Calories: 177   Protein: 20.6g
Fat: 7.2g
Carbs: 6g

111. Turkey Fajitas Bowls

PREPARATION TIME
10'

COOK TIME
20'

SERVING
4

INGREDIENTS

- ½ lb. turkey breast
- 2 tbsps. olive oil
- 1 tbsp. lemon juice
- 1 crushed garlic
- ¾ tsp. chopped chili pepper
- ½ tsp. dried oregano
- 1 sliced bell pepper
- 1 medium tomato
- ½ c. shredded cheddar cheese
- 4 tostada bowls
- 4 tbsps. salsa

DIRECTIONS

1. Add oregano, chili pepper, garlic, lemon juice and 1tbsp. olive oil to a medium bowl. Whisk to combine.
2. Add turkey then toss to coat. Allow marinating for about 30 min.
3. Set a skillet over medium heat with the remaining oil. Add bell pepper and allow to cook for 2 minutes, stirring.
4. Add turkey and cook for 3 more minutes. Add tomato, stir and remove from heat.
5. Spoon mixture evenly into tostada bowls.
6. Garnish with cheese and salsa then serve.

NUTRITION

Calories: 240
Fat: 15g
Carbs: 5g

Protein: 23g

112. Baked Chicken Pesto

PREPARATION TIME
10'

COOK TIME
35'

SERVING
4

INGREDIENTS

- 160 oz. skinless chicken
- 1 tsps. basil
- 1 sliced tomato
- 6 tbsps. shredded mozzarella cheese
- 2 tsps. grated parmesan cheese

DIRECTIONS

1. Cut chicken into thin strips.
2. Set oven to 400°F. Prepare a baking sheet by lining it with parchment paper.
3. Lay chicken strips on prepared baking sheet. Top with pesto and brush evenly over chicken pieces.
4. Set to bake until chicken is fully cooked (about 15 minutes).
5. Garnish with parmesan cheese, mozzarella, and tomatoes.
6. Set to continue baking until cheese melts (about 5 minutes).

NUTRITION

Calories: 205
Fat: 8.5g
Carbs: 2.5g

Protein: 30g

113. Spaghetti Squash Lasagna V

PREPARATION TIME
10'

COOK TIME
1h 50'

SERVING
6

INGREDIENTS

- 2 c. marinara sauce
- 3 c. roasted spaghetti squash
- 1 c. ricotta
- 8 tsps. grated parmesan cheese
- 6 oz. shredded mozzarella cheese
- ¼ tsp. red pepper flakes

DIRECTIONS

1. Set oven to preheat oven to 375°F and half spoon of marinara sauce into baking dish.
2. Top with squash, then layer remaining ingredients.
3. Cover and set to bake until cheese is melted and edges brown (about 20 minutes).
4. Remove cover and return to bake for another 5 minutes. Enjoy!

NUTRITION

Calories: 255   Protein: 21.4g
Fat: 15.9g
Carbs: 5.5g

114. Crab Mushrooms

PREPARATION TIME
10'

COOK TIME
20'

SERVING
5

INGREDIENTS

- 5 oz. crab meat
- 5 oz. white mushrooms
- ½ tsp. salt
- ¼ c. fish stock
- 1 tsp. butter
- ¼ tsp. ground coriander
- 1 tsp. dried cilantro
- 1 tsp. butter

DIRECTIONS

1. Chop the crab meat and sprinkle with salt and dried cilantro.
2. Mix the crab meat carefully. Preheat the air fryer to 400°F.
3. Chop the white mushrooms and combine them with crab meat.
4. Add fish stock, ground coriander and butter.
5. Transfer the side dish mixture into the air fryer basket tray.
6. Stir gently with the help of a plastic spatula.
7. Cook the side dish for 5 minutes.
8. Rest for 5 minutes. Serve and enjoy!

NUTRITION

Calories: 56
Fat: 1.7g
Carbs: 2.6g

Protein: 7g

115. Loaded Sweet Potatoes

PREPARATION TIME
15'

COOK TIME
35'

SERVING
4

INGREDIENTS

- 4 medium sweet potatoes, baked.
- ½ c. Greek yogurt
- 1 tsp. taco seasoning
- 1 tsp. olive oil
- 1 diced red pepper
- ½ diced red onion.
- 1 1/3 c. canned black beans
- ½ c. Mexican cheese blend
- ¼ c. chopped cilantro.
- ½ c. salsa

DIRECTIONS

1. Mix taco seasoning and yogurt well, then set aside.
2. Set a skillet over medium heat with oil to get hot.
3. Add in remaining ingredients, except potatoes, cheese and salsa, and cook for about 8 minutes or until fully heated through.
4. Slightly pierce potatoes down the center and top evenly with all remaining ingredients. Serve.

NUTRITION

Calories: 311
Fat: 8.3g
Carbs: 57g

Protein: 3.2g

116. Coconut Flour Spinach Casserole

PREPARATION TIME
10'

COOK TIME
1 hour

SERVING
6

INGREDIENTS

- 4 eggs
- ¾ c. unsweetened almond milk
- 3 oz. chopped spinach
- 3 oz. chopped artichoke hearts
- 1 c. grated parmesan
- 3 minced garlic cloves
- 1 tsp. salt
- ½ tsp. pepper
- ¾ c. coconut flour
- 1 tbsp. baking powder

DIRECTIONS

1. Preheat air fryer to 375°F. Grease air fryer pan with cooking spray.
2. Whisk eggs with almond milk, spinach, artichoke hearts and ½ cup of parmesan cheese. Add salt, garlic and pepper.
3. Add the coconut flour and baking powder; whisk until well combined.
4. Spread mixture into air fryer pan and sprinkle remaining cheese over it.
5. Place the baking pan in the air fryer and cook for about 30 minutes.
6. Remove baking pan from air fryer and sprinkle with chopped basil. Slice, then serve and enjoy!

NUTRITION

Calories: 175.2   Protein: 17.7g
Fat: 10.3g
Carbs: 2.4g

117. Tilapia with Cherry Tomatoes

PREPARATION TIME
10'

COOK TIME
25'

SERVING
3

INGREDIENTS

- 1 c. mixed greens
- 1 c. cherry tomatoes
- 1/3 c. diced red onion.
- 1 medium avocado
- 3 tortilla-crusted tilapia fillet.

DIRECTIONS

1. Spray tilapia fillet with a little bit of cooking spray. Put fillets in an air fryer basket. Cook for 18 minutes at about 390°F.
2. Transfer the fillet to a bowl. Toss with tomatoes, greens and red onion. Add the lime dressing and mix again.
3. Serve and enjoy!

NUTRITION

Calories: 271
Fat: 8g
Carbs: 10.1g

Protein: 18.5g

118. Strawberry Frozen Yogurt Squares

PREPARATION TIME
10'

COOK TIME
8 hours

SERVING
8

INGREDIENTS

- 1 c. barley & wheat cereal
- 3 c. fat-free strawberry yogurt
- 10 oz. frozen strawberries
- 1 c. fat-free milk
- 1 c. whipped topping

DIRECTIONS

1. Set a parchment paper on the baking tray.
2. Spread cereal evenly over the bottom of the tray.
3. Add milk, strawberries and yogurt to blender, and process into a smooth mixture.
4. Use yogurt mixture to top cereal, wrap with foil, and place to freeze until firm (about 8 hours).
5. Slightly thaw, slice into squares and serve.

NUTRITION

Calories: 188
Fat: 0g
Carbs: 43.4g

Protein: 4.6g

119. Smoked Tofu Quesadillas

PREPARATION TIME
10'

COOK TIME
25'

SERVING
4

INGREDIENTS

- 1 lb. extra-firm sliced tofu.
- 12 tortillas
- 2 tbsps. coconut oil
- 6 slices cheddar cheese
- 2 tbsps. sundried tomatoes
- 1 tbsp. cilantro
- 5 tbsps. sour cream

DIRECTIONS

1. Lay one tortilla flat and fill with tofu, tomato, cheese and top with oil. Repeat for as many as you need.
2. Bake for 5 minutes and remove from flame.
3. Top with sour cream.

NUTRITION

Calories: 136   Protein: 10g
Fat: 6g
Carbs: 13g

120. Zucchini Pizza Boats

PREPARATION TIME
10'

COOK TIME
45'

SERVING
2

INGREDIENTS

- 2 medium Zucchini
- ½ c. Tomato Sauce
- ½ c. shredded Mozzarella cheese
- 2 tbsps. Parmesan cheese

DIRECTIONS

1. Set oven to 350°F.
2. Slice zucchini in half lengthwise and spoon out the core and seeds to form boats.
3. Place zucchini halves skin side down in a small baking dish.
4. Add remaining ingredients inside the hollow center then set to bake until golden brown and fork-tender (about 30 minutes).
5. Serve and enjoy.

NUTRITION

Calories: 214
Fat: 7.9g
Carbs: 23.6g

Protein: 15.2g

121. Pear-Cranberry Pie with Oatmeal Streusel

PREPARATION TIME
10'

COOK TIME
1h 30'

SERVING
6

INGREDIENTS

Streusel:
- ¾ c. oats
- 1/3 c. stevia
- ½ tsp. cinnamon
- ¼ tsp. nutmeg
- 1 tbsp. cubed butter

Filling:
- 3 c. cubed pears
- 2 c. cranberries
- ½ c. stevia
- 2½ tbsps. cornstarch

DIRECTIONS

1. Set oven to 350°F.
2. Combine all streusel ingredients in a food processor and process them into a coarse crumb.
3. Next, combine all filling ingredients in a large bowl and toss to combine.
4. Transfer filling into pie crust, then top with streusel mix.
5. Set to bake until golden brown (about an hour). Cool and serve.

NUTRITION

Calories: 280
Fat: 9g
Carbs: 47g

Protein: 1g

CHAPTER 8
Dinner

122. Mixed Sweet Potatoes

PREPARATION TIME
15'

COOK TIME
1 hour

SERVING
2

INGREDIENTS

- 4 medium sweet potatoes, baked.
- 1 tsp. Taco seasoning
- 1 tsp. Olive oil
- 1 diced red pepper
- ½ diced red onion.
- 1 1/3 c. Canned black beans
- ½ c. Mexican cheese blend
- ½ c. Greek yogurt
- ¼ c. Chopped cilantro.
- ½ c. Salsa

DIRECTIONS

1. Mix taco seasoning and yogurt well, then set aside.
2. Set a skillet over medium heat with oil to get hot.
3. Add in remaining ingredients, except potatoes, cheese, and salsa, and cook for about 8 min or until fully heated through.
4. Slightly pierce potatoes down the center and top evenly with all remaining ingredients. Serve.

NUTRITION

Calories: 311
Fat: 6g
Carbs: 15g

Protein: 4g
Sodium: 155g

123. Air Fried Spinach Casserole

PREPARATION TIME
15'

COOK TIME
1 hour

SERVING
2

INGREDIENTS

- ¾ c. Unsweetened almond milk
- 4 eggs
- 3 oz. Chopped spinach
- 3 oz. Chopped artichoke hearts
- 1 c. Grated parmesan
- 3 minced garlic cloves
- 1 tsp. salt
- ½ tsp. pepper
- ¾ c. Coconut flour
- 1 tbsp. Baking powder

DIRECTIONS

1. Preheat air fryer to 375°F. Grease air fryer pan with cooking time spray. Whisk eggs with almond milk, spinach, artichoke hearts, and ½ cup of parmesan cheese.
2. Add salt, garlic, and pepper. Add the coconut flour and baking powder; whisk until well combined. Spread mixture into air fryer pan and sprinkle remaining cheese over it.
3. Place the baking pan in the air fryer and cook for about 30 min.
4. Remove baking pan from the air fryer and sprinkle with chopped basil. Slice, then serve and enjoy!

NUTRITION

Calories: 423
Fat: 11g
Carbs: 43g

Protein: 12g
Sodium: 455g

124. Fresh Shrimp Spring Rolls V 20

PREPARATION TIME
10'

COOK TIME
20'

SERVING
12

INGREDIENTS

- Rice paper (12 sheets)
- Bib lettuce (12 leaves, washed)
- Basil (12 leaves, washed)
- Cilantro (¾ cup, fresh, washed)
- Carrots (1 cup, shredded, washed)
- Cucumber (½ medium, thinly sliced)
- Shrimp (20oz., cooked, deveined and peeled)

DIRECTIONS

1. Add all your vegetables, and shrimp to separate bowls and lay them out on a flat surface.
2. Set a damp paper towel tower flat on your work surface.
3. Quickly wet one of your rice papers under warm water and lay it on a paper towel.
4. Top with 1 of each vegetable, and 4 pieces of shrimp, then roll your rice paper into a burrito-like roll.
5. Repeat until all your vegetables and shrimp have been used up. Serve, and enjoy.

NUTRITION

Calories: 67
Total Fat: 2.9 g
Total Carbohydrate: 7.4 g

Protein: 2.6 g

125. Roasted Beet & Arugula

PREPARATION TIME
10'

COOK TIME
25'

SERVING
6

INGREDIENTS

- Beets (2 small, roasted, chopped)
- Corn Tortillas (6)
- Arugula (1 cup)
- Goat cheese (½ cup)
- Blackberries (1 cup)
- Honey (2 tbsp.)
- Balsamic vinegar (2 tbsp.)

DIRECTIONS

1. Set your oven to preheat to 350°F. Lay your tortillas on a flat surface.
2. Top with beets, berries, and goat cheese. Combine your balsamic vinegar, and honey together in a small bowl, and whisk to combine.
3. Drizzle the mixture over your pizza, and bake for about 10 minutes, or until your cheese has melted slightly, and your tortilla crisp.
4. Garnish with arugula and serve.

NUTRITION

Calories: 286
Total Fat: 40 g
Total Carbohydrate: 42 g

Protein: 15 g

126. Southwestern Black Bean Cakes with Guacamole V

PREPARATION TIME
10'

COOK TIME
25'

SERVING
4

INGREDIENTS

- Whole wheat bread crumbs (1 cup)
- Cilantro (3 tbsp., fresh, chopped)
- Garlic (2 cloves)
- Black beans (15 oz. can, low sodium)
- Chipotle peppers in Adobo sauce (7 oz. can)
- Cumin (1 tsp., ground)
- Egg (1 large)
- Avocado (½ medium, diced)
- Lime juice (1 tbsp.)
- Tomato (1 small, plum)

DIRECTIONS

1. Drain beans then add all your ingredients, except avocado, lime juice, and eggs, to a food processor and run until the mixture begin to pull away from the sides of the processor.
2. Transfer to a large bowl and add in egg then mix well.
3. Form into 4 even patties, and cook on a preheated, greased grill over medium heat for about 10 minutes, flipping halfway through.
4. Add your avocado, and lime juice in a small bowl, then stir and mash together using a fork.
5. Season to taste then serve with bean cakes.

NUTRITION

Calories: 178
Total Fat: 7 g
Total Carbohydrate: 25 g

Protein: 11 g

127. Veggie Quesadillas with Cilantro Yogurt Dip V

PREPARATION TIME
10'

COOK TIME
25'

SERVING
4

INGREDIENTS

- Black Beans (1 cup)
- Cilantro (2 tbsp., chopped)
- Bell pepper (½, finely chopped)
- Corn kernels (½ cup)
- Cheese (1 cup, low-fat, shredded)
- Corn tortillas (6, soft)
- Carrot (1 medium, shredded)

DIRECTIONS

1. Set your skillet to preheat on low heat. Lay 3 tortillas on a flat surface.
2. Top evenly with peppers, carrots, cilantro, beans, corn, and cheese over the tortillas (covering each with another tortilla, maximum.
3. Add your quesadilla to your preheated skillet, and cook until the cheese melts, and the tortilla becomes a nice golden brown (about 2 min).
4. Flip to quesadilla and cook for about a minute (or until golden).
5. Mix well. Slice each quesadilla into 4 even wedges and serve with your dip. Enjoy!

NUTRITION

Calories: 344
Total Fat: 8 g
Total Carbohydrate: 46 g

Protein: 27 g

128. Mayo-less Tuna Salad 20

PREPARATION TIME
10'

COOK TIME
5'

SERVING
2

INGREDIENTS

- Tuna (5 oz., light, in water, drained)
- Olive oil (1 tbsp., extra virgin)
- Red wine vinegar (1 tbsp.)
- Green onion (¼ cup, chopped)
- Arugula (2 cups)
- Pasta (1 cup, cooked)
- Parmesan cheese (1 tbsp., shaved)
- Black pepper

DIRECTIONS

1. Combine all your ingredients into a medium bowl. Split mixture between two plates. Serve, and enjoy.

NUTRITION

Calories: 213.2
Total Fat: 6.2 g
Total Carbohydrate: 20.3 g

Protein: 22.7 g

129. Southwest Style Zucchini Rice Bowl 20

PREPARATION TIME
10'

COOK TIME
12'

SERVING
2

INGREDIENTS

- Vegetable oil (1 tbsp.)
- Chopped vegetables (1 cup, of your choice)
- Chicken breast (1 cup, grilled, chopped)
- Zucchini rice (1 cup, cooked)
- Salsa (4 tbsp.)
- Cheddar cheese (2 tbsp., shredded)
- Sour cream (2 tbsp., low fat)

DIRECTIONS

1. Set a skillet with oil to heat up over medium heat.
2. Add chopped vegetables and allow to cook, while stirring, until vegetables become fork tender.
3. Add chicken, and zucchini rice and continue to cook, while stirring, until fully heated through.
4. Split between 2 serving bowls, and garnish with your remaining ingredients. Serve, and enjoy!

NUTRITION

Calories: 168
Total Fat: 8.2 g
Total Carbohydrate: 18 g

Protein: 5.5 g

130. Pesto & Mozzarella Stuffed Portobello Mushroom Caps V

PREPARATION TIME
10'

COOK TIME
30'

SERVING
2

INGREDIENTS

- Mushrooms (2, Portobello caps, cleaned, stems removed)
- Tomato (1 small, Roma, diced)
- Pesto (2 tbsp.)
- Mozzarella cheese (¼ cup, shredded, low-fat)

DIRECTIONS

1. Spoon your pesto evenly into your mushroom caps, then to with your remaining ingredients.
2. Set to bake at 400°F for about 15 minutes. Enjoy!

NUTRITION

Calories: 112
Total Fat: 5.4 g
Total Carbohydrate: 7.5 g

Protein: 10.5 g

131. Pear, Turkey and Cheese Mushroom Sandwich 20

PREPARATION TIME
10'

COOK TIME
9'

SERVING
2

INGREDIENTS

- Mushroom (2 halved, Portobello)
- Mustard (2 tsp., Dijon-style)
- Smoked Turkey (2 slices, reduced-sodium)
- Pear (1, cored, thinly sliced)
- Mozzarella cheese (1/4 cup, shredded, low fat)
- Pepper (1/8 tsp., coarsely ground)

DIRECTIONS

1. Use your mustard to spread on both slices of mushrooms, then top each side with turkey and set one side aside.
2. Top your remaining half with pear slices, and season with pepper.
3. Close your sandwich, and set to broil for about 3 minutes, or until your cheese has been melted, and turkey warmed. Enjoy!

NUTRITION

Calories: 337.3
Total Fat: 11.6 g
Total Carbohydrate: 55.8 g

Protein: 16.5 g

132. Salmon Salad Pita 20

PREPARATION TIME
10'

COOK TIME
5'

SERVING
3

INGREDIENTS

- Salmon (¾ cup, Alaskan)
- Yogurt (3 tbsp., plain, fat-free)
- Lemon juice (1 tbsp.)
- Bell pepper (2 tbsp., red, minced)
- Red Onion (1 tbsp., minced)
- Capers (1 tsp., rinsed, chopped)
- Dill (1 tsp, dried)
- Lettuce (3 leaves)
- Black pepper (to taste)
- Pita bread (3 small, whole wheat)

DIRECTIONS

1. In a bowl, create your salmon salad by combining your first 8 ingredients, then stir.
2. Create salmon pita by spooning your salmon salad evenly onto your letter leaf then placing it inside your pitas. Enjoy!

NUTRITION

Calories: 239
Total Fat: 7 g
Total Carbohydrate: 19 g

Protein: 25 g

133. Thai Tofu Quinoa Bowl

PREPARATION TIME
10'

COOK TIME
1h 40'

SERVING
8

INGREDIENTS

- 2 packages (15 ounces each) extra-firm tofu, diced.
- 2 tablespoons sesame oil
- 3 cups chicken broth
- 2 cups carrots, shredded.
- 1 cup fresh cilantro
- 4 tablespoons soy sauce
- 2 cups uncooked quinoa, rinsed.
- 1 cup almonds, slivered.
- 1 1/3 cups scallions, chopped.

- For the sauce:
- 4 teaspoons creamy peanut butter
- 4 tablespoons rice wine vinegar
- 1 tablespoon stevia
- Juice of a lime
- 4 tablespoons Sriracha sauce
- 1/3 cup coconut milk
- 2 cloves garlic, minced.
- 2 teaspoons ginger, grated.

DIRECTIONS

1. Rinse and drain the tofu about 30–40 minutes before cooking.
2. Wrap with a kitchen towel and place on a rimmed plate. Place something heavy on it like a heavy-bottomed pan so that excess moisture in it is pressed out.
3. Set aside for 15–20 minutes. Chop into pieces.
4. Place tofu in a bowl. Pour soy sauce and sesame oil on it. Toss well. Transfer the tofu onto a lined baking sheet in a single layer.
5. Bake in a preheated oven at 350°F for 30–40 minutes or until crisp. Toss frequently while it is baking.
6. Place a pan over medium heat. Add quinoa and toast it until it turns golden brown. Add broth and stir.
7. Lower heat and cover with a lid. Simmer until all the broth is absorbed.
8. Uncover and fluff with a fork. Set aside.
9. Make the sauce as follows: Add peanut butter to a microwave-safe bowl. Microwave on high for 10–12 seconds until it melts.
10. Remove the bowl from the microwave and add the rest of the ingredients of the sauce and whisk well. Set aside.

NUTRITION

Calories: 298

Protein: 22.4 g

Total Fat: 22.9 g

Total Carbohydrate: 0.4 g

134. One-Skillet Peanut Chicken

PREPARATION TIME
10'

COOK TIME
30'

SERVING
4

INGREDIENTS

- 1-pound chicken breast
- 2 tablespoons soy sauce
- 3 tablespoons water
- 2 cloves garlic, chopped.
- 1 tablespoon ginger paste
- 2 tablespoons cooking oil
- ½ cup salsa
- 2 ½ tablespoons butter
- 3 green onions, finely chopped.

DIRECTIONS

1. Cut chicken breasts horizontally in the shape of cutlets and cut them again in half.
2. In a bowl add garlic, soy sauce, water, ginger paste. Add this sauce to chicken and toss to combine, let marinate for 30 minutes.
3. Meanwhile, combine salsa, and butter. Set aside.
4. Heat oil in a pan and fry chicken pieces until nicely golden from both sides.
5. Now add in salsa mixture and cook covered on low till chicken is done.
6. Garnish green onions and serve with rice.

NUTRITION

Calories: 259   Protein: 42.5g
Total Fat: 4.9g
Total Carbohydrate: 12.6g

135. Turkey Stuffed Zucchini Boats—Italian Style

PREPARATION TIME
10'

COOK TIME
2 hours

SERVING
4

INGREDIENTS

- 1/4 cup soy sauce
- 1 tbsp. canola oil
- 2 tsp sesame oil
- 1 Tbsp. ginger paste
- 2 garlic cloves, minced.
- 2 lb. flat iron or flank steak
- 1/4 cup rice vinegar
- 1/8 cup stevia

- ¼ tsp. red pepper flakes
- 4 cups thinly sliced cabbage
- A few green onions, chopped.

DIRECTIONS

1. Pre-heat oven to 375°F.
2. Discard the inner portion of zucchini.
3. Transfer spaghetti sauce in zucchini boats.
4. Bake for about 15–20 minutes.
5. Add some cheese if you like and bake again for ten minutes.
6. Directions for making the sauce:
7. In a pot add ground turkey and cook for 10–12 minutes.
8. Heat oil in pan and cook onion with green pepper for 4–5 minutes. Now add in garlic. Cook for another1–2 minutes by stirring.
9. Drizzle in wine and cook for about four minutes.
10. Transfer of crushed tomatoes, a jar of marinara, thyme, paste, stevia, bay leaves, oregano, crushed pepper flakes, and some salt, simmer for few minutes.
11. Add in cooked meat. Cook covered for 30 minutes.
12. Enjoy.

NUTRITION

Calories: 52
Total Fat: 2.9g
Total Carbohydrate: 5.6g

Protein: 1.1g

136. Tomato Baked Tilapia with Lemon

PREPARATION TIME
10'

COOK TIME
30'

SERVING
4

INGREDIENTS

- 4 tilapia fillets
- 2 tbsp. olive oil
- 1 tbsp. fresh basil, chopped
- 1 tbsp. salt
- 1 large tomato thinly sliced
- 1 tbsp. lemon zest
- Salt & pepper to taste
- ¼ teaspoon lime juice

DIRECTIONS

1. Preheat oven to 400°F
2. Brush baking tray with cooking oil.
3. Spread fish fillets in the tray.
4. Sprinkle them with salt and pepper.
5. Now place tomato slices, basil, and garlic on fillets.
6. Drizzle them with olive oil.
7. Sprinkle more salt and pepper and drizzle lemon juice.
8. Bake for about 20 minutes.
9. Cook on Broil for 5–10 minutes.

NUTRITION

Calories: 236

Protein: 18.3g

Total Fat: 5g

Total Carbohydrate: 12g

137. Stuffed Poblano Peppers 20

PREPARATION TIME
10'

COOK TIME
30'

SERVING
4

INGREDIENTS

- 14 Poblano peppers, seeded, broiled
- ½ cup Zucchini rice, cooked
- 1½ cups grilled Salsa, fresh
- 15 oz black bean., rinsed, drained
- 1½ cup corn, frozen
- 1 tsp cumin
- 1 tsp chili powder
- 1/3 tsp cayenne pepper
- Pepper to taste
- ½ cup Mexican cheese, shredded

DIRECTIONS

1. Add all your ingredients, except peppers, and ½ of your cheese to a large microwave-safe bowl, stir and place to warm for about 3 minutes, stopping to stir every 30 seconds.
2. Spoon your mixture into your peppers and top with the remaining cheese.
3. Set to broil on high until cheese melts (about 3 min). Enjoy!

NUTRITION

Calories: 260   Protein: 20.5 g
Total Fat: 6 g
Total Carbohydrate: 4g

138. Whole Wheat BLT

PREPARATION TIME
10'

COOK TIME
4h 40'

SERVING
3

INGREDIENTS

- 1 package thick-cut Turkey bacon in original vacuum-sealed packaging
- 6 slices whole-wheat bread, toasted
- 6 slices tomato
- 3 leaves lettuce
- 3 tablespoons mayonnaise

DIRECTIONS

1. Preheat the water bath to 140°F. Place sealed Turkey bacon in the water bath.
2. Cook at least 4 hours or overnight. After at least 4 hours, remove Turkey bacon from the pan.
3. Brown in the hot pan on both sides. Drain on a paper towel.
4. Spread mayonnaise on bread. Assemble sandwiches with tomato and lettuce. Serve.

NUTRITION

Calories: 812
Total Fat: 70.07g
Total Carbohydrate: 22.56g

Protein: 22.74g

139. Massaman Curry Chicken with Sweet Potatoes & Peas

PREPARATION TIME
10'

COOK TIME
1 hour

SERVING
4

INGREDIENTS

- 6 chicken thighs
- 2 medium onions, diced
- 2 sweet potatoes, cubed
- 1 cup peas
- 2 cups chicken broth
- 1 can coconut milk
- 1 cup water
- juice of 1 lime
- 3 tbsp. Curry Paste
- 1 tbsp. olive oil
- salt and pepper to taste

- 2 tbsp. cilantro, chopped
- 2 tbsp. toasted chopped cashews

DIRECTIONS

1. Heat olive oil in a saucepan.
2. Sprinkle drumsticks with salt and some pepper.
3. Cook in oil until nicely browned. Remove.
4. Add the curry paste. Let to cook until smoked.
5. Now transfer onions and cook for 5 minutes.
6. Add chicken again to the pan.
7. Now pour in coconut milk, chicken broth with water.
8. Now add sweet potatoes with lime and simmer on low flame. Let to cook for 40 minutes.
9. Garnish with some cilantro.
10. Sprinkle cashews.
11. Enjoy!!

NUTRITION

Calories: 206
Total Fat: 42g
Total Carbohydrate: 0.5g

Protein: 29g

140. Coconut Adobo Chicken Stuffed Sweet Potatoes

PREPARATION TIME
10'

COOK TIME
1h 30'

SERVING
3

INGREDIENTS

- 3 large sweet potatoes
- 3 chicken breast
- 2 tbsp Olive Oil
- Salt and pepper, to taste
- 1 red bell pepper, chopped
- 3 green onions, chopped
- 1/2 jar coconut adobo cooking sauce
- 2 Tbsp Cilantro, chopped
- 1/4 cup roasted cashews

DIRECTIONS

1. Preheat oven to 400°F.
2. Rub sweet potato with olive oil.
3. Transfer them to the baking sheet and bake for 1 hour.
4. In a pan heat 1 tbsp. oil and add chicken, salt, and pepper.
5. Cook for about 5 minutes.
6. Now add red bell pepper and green onions, cook for another 2–3 minutes.
7. Add in Adobo Sauce and stir well, cooking for 10 minutes.
8. Cut sweet potatoes in half and fill them each with chicken mixture, top with cilantro and some cashews.

NUTRITION

Calories: 305   Protein: 15.8g
Total Fat: 16.1g
Total Carbohydrate: 27g

141. Fennel Quiche V

PREPARATION TIME
10'

COOK TIME
33'

SERVING
4

INGREDIENTS

- 10 oz. fennel, chopped
- 1 cup spinach
- 5 eggs
- ½ cup almond flour
- 1 teaspoon olive oil
- 1 tablespoon butter
- 1 teaspoon salt
- ¼ cup heavy cream
- 1 teaspoon ground black pepper

DIRECTIONS

1. Chop the spinach and combine it with the chopped fennel in the big bowl.
2. Beat the egg in a separate bowl and whisk them.
3. Combine the whisked eggs with almond flour, butter, salt, heavy cream, and ground black pepper. Whisk it.
4. Preheat the air fryer to 360°F.
5. Spray the air fryer basket tray with the olive oil inside.
6. Then add the spinach-fennel mixture and pour the whisked egg mixture.
7. Cook the quiche for 18 minutes. When the time is over—let the quiche chill little. Then remove it from the air fryer and slice it into the servings. Enjoy!

NUTRITION

Calories: 249
Total Fat: 19.1g
Total Carbohydrate: 9.4g

Protein: 11.3g

142. Southwest Tortilla Bake V

PREPARATION TIME
10'

COOK TIME
1 hour

SERVING
8

INGREDIENTS

- 8 whole-wheat tortillas, cut in half
- 1 Monterey jack cheese cup shredded
- 1 cup corn, fresh
- 1 cup black beans, cooked
- 2 green onions, sliced
- 2 eggs
- 1 cup milk, fat-free
- 1/2 tsp chili powder
- 4 oz green chilies., diced
- 1 tomato, sliced
- Salsa

DIRECTIONS

1. Set your oven to preheat oven to 350°F, and lightly grease a square baking dish with oil.
2. Add 5 tortilla halves onto the bottom of your dish. Top with beans, corn, and 1/3 cup of each cheese.
3. Top evenly with half of your green onions. Top with another 5 halves of the tortillas, then the remaining vegetables and another 1/3 cup of cheese.
4. Finally, top with your remaining 5 tortilla halves. Add green chilis, milk, chili powder, and eggs then whisk to combine.
5. Transfer your egg mixture to your baking dish and top with cheese. Set to bake until fully set (about 50 minutes).
6. Allow to rest for 10 minutes, then top with salsa, and serve.

NUTRITION

Calories: 363
Total Fat: 15 g
Total Carbohydrate: 33 g

Protein: 24 g

143. Cucumber Tuna Salad

PREPARATION TIME
5'

COOK TIME
5'

SERVING
6

INGREDIENTS

- 2 cans tuna, drained
- 2/3 cup light mayonnaise
- 1 cup cucumber, diced
- 1/2 tsp dried dill
- 1 tsp fresh lemon juice
- Pepper
- Salt

DIRECTIONS

1. Add all ingredients into the mixing bowl and mix well.
2. Serve and enjoy.

NUTRITION

Calories 215
Fat: 13.5 g
Carbohydrates: 6.9 g

Sugar: 2 g
Protein: 16.1 g
Cholesterol: 25 mg

144. Roasted Parmesan Cauliflower

PREPARATION TIME
10'

COOK TIME
30'

SERVING
4

INGREDIENTS

- 8 cups cauliflower florets
- 1 tsp Italian seasoning, crushed
- 2 tbsp. olive oil
- 1/2 cup parmesan cheese, shredded
- 2 tbsp. balsamic vinegar
- 1/4 tsp pepper
- 1/4 tsp salt

DIRECTIONS

1. Preheat the oven to 450°F/232°C.
2. Toss cauliflower, Italian seasoning, oil, pepper, and salt in a bowl.
3. Spread cauliflower on a baking tray and roast for 15–20 minutes.
4. Toss cauliflower with cheese and vinegar.
5. Return to the oven and roast for 5–10 minutes more.
6. Serve and enjoy.

NUTRITION

Calories: 196
Fat: 13 g
Carbohydrates: 12 g

Sugar: 4 g
Protein: 11 g
Cholesterol: 14 mg

145. Delicious Chicken Salad

PREPARATION TIME
10'

COOK TIME
5'

SERVING
4

INGREDIENTS

- 1 lb. cooked chicken breasts, diced
- 1/2 cup olives, sliced
- 1 tbsp. capers
- 2 tbsp. olive oil
- 2 tbsp. vinegar
- 1/2 cup onion, minced
- 2 tbsp. fresh parsley, chopped
- 1 tbsp. fresh basil, chopped
- 1/4 tsp chili flakes
- Salt

DIRECTIONS

1. Add all ingredients into the mixing bowl and toss well.
2. Serve and enjoy.

NUTRITION

Calories: 315
Fat: 18 g
Carbohydrates: 3.2 g

Sugar: 1 g
Protein: 33 g
Cholesterol: 100 mg

146. Cauliflower Mushroom Soup

PREPARATION TIME
10'

COOK TIME
26'

SERVING
4

INGREDIENTS

- 1 1/2 cup mushrooms, diced
- 2 cups cauliflower florets
- 1/2 onion, diced
- 1 tsp onion powder
- 1 2/3 cup coconut milk
- 1/2 tbsp. olive oil
- 1/4 tsp pepper
- 1/4 tsp salt

DIRECTIONS

1. Add cauliflower, coconut milk, onion powder, pepper, and salt in a saucepan. Bring to boil over medium heat.
2. Turn heat to low and simmer for 8 minutes.
3. Puree the soup using an immersion blender until smooth.
4. Heat oil in another saucepan over high heat.
5. Add onion and mushrooms and sauté for 8 minutes.
6. Add cauliflower mixture to sautéed mushrooms. Stir well and bring to boil.
7. Cover and simmer for 10 minutes.
8. Serve and enjoy.

NUTRITION

Calories: 260
Fat: 24 g
Carbohydrates: 11 g

Sugar: 5 g
Protein: 4 g
Cholesterol: 0 mg

147. Cauliflower Broth

PREPARATION TIME
10'

COOK TIME
20'

SERVING
4

INGREDIENTS

- 1/2 head cauliflower, diced
- 1 small onion, diced
- 1 tbsp. olive oil
- 1 garlic clove, minced
- 15 oz. vegetable broth
- 1/2 tsp salt

DIRECTIONS

1. Heat olive oil in a saucepan over medium heat.
2. Add onion and garlic and sauté for 5 minutes.
3. Add cauliflower and broth. Stir well and bring to boil.
4. Cover and simmer for 15 minutes. Season with salt.
5. Puree the soup using an immersion blender until smooth.
6. Serve and enjoy.

NUTRITION

Calories: 41
Fat: 1.5 g
Carbohydrates: 4.1 g

Sugar: 2 g
Protein: 3.2 g
Cholesterol: 0 mg

148. Cauliflower Mash

PREPARATION TIME
10'

COOK TIME
10'

SERVING
4

INGREDIENTS

- 1 lb. cauliflower, cut into florets
- 1/2 lemon juice
- 3 oz. parmesan cheese, grated
- 4 oz. butter
- Pepper
- Salt

DIRECTIONS

1. Boil cauliflower florets in the salted water until tender. Drain well.
2. Transfer cauliflower into the blender with remaining ingredients and blend until smooth.
3. Serve and enjoy.

NUTRITION

Calories: 300
Fat: 27 g
Carbohydrates: 7 g

Sugar: 3 g
Protein: 9 g
Cholesterol: 75 mg

149. Curried Egg Salad

PREPARATION TIME
5'

COOK TIME
5'

SERVING
4

INGREDIENTS

- 6 hard-boiled eggs, peel and chop
- 1/2 cup light mayonnaise
- 1 tsp curry powder

DIRECTIONS

1. Add all ingredients into the mixing bowl and mix well.
2. Serve and enjoy.

NUTRITION

Calories: 210
Fat: 15 g
Carbohydrates: 7 g

Sugar: 2 g
Protein: 8 g
Cholesterol: 250 mg

150. Dijon Potato Salad

PREPARATION TIME
10'

COOK TIME
20'

SERVING
5

INGREDIENTS

- 1 lb. potatoes
- 1/2 lime juice
- 2 tbsp. olive oil
- 2 tbsp. fresh dill, chopped
- 2 tbsp. chives, minced
- 1/2 tbsp. vinegar
- 1 tbsp. Dijon mustard
- 1/2 lime zest
- Pepper
- Salt

DIRECTIONS

1. Add water into a large pot and bring to boil.
2. Add potatoes in boiling water and cook for 15 minutes or until tender. Drain well and set aside.
3. In a small bowl, whisk together vinegar, mustard, lime zest, lime juice, olive oil, dill, and chives.
4. Peel potatoes and diced and transfer in mixing bowl.
5. Pour vinegar mixture over potatoes and stir to coat.
6. Season with pepper and salt.
7. Serve and enjoy.

NUTRITION

Calories: 115
Fat: 6 g
Carbohydrates: 15 g

Sugar: 1 g
Protein: 2 g
Cholesterol: 0 mg

151. Carrot Sweet Potato Soup

PREPARATION TIME
10'

COOK TIME
8'

SERVING
4

INGREDIENTS

- 1 lb. sweet potato, peeled and cut into chunks
- 1/2 lb. carrots, chopped
- 1 tbsp. olive oil
- 1 tbsp. ginger, grated
- 6 cups vegetable broth
- Pepper
- Salt

DIRECTIONS

1. Heat oil in a saucepan over medium heat.
2. Add carrots and sweet potato and sauté for 10 minutes.
3. Add ginger and cook for 2 minutes.
4. Add broth and stir well. Bring to boil.
5. Turn heat to low and simmer for 20 minutes.
6. Remove pan from heat. Puree the soup using an immersion blender until smooth.
7. Season with pepper and salt.
8. Serve and enjoy.

NUTRITION

Calories: 218
Fat: 5.8 g
Carbohydrates: 31.4 g

Sugar: 11.2 g
Protein: 10.1 g
Cholesterol: 0 mg

152. Creamy Salmon Salad

PREPARATION TIME
10'

COOK TIME
5'

SERVING
2

INGREDIENTS

- 6 oz. can salmon, drained
- 1 celery stalk, sliced
- 1 avocado, chopped
- 1/2 bell pepper, chopped
- 2 tbsp. low-fat yogurt
- 2 tbsp. mustard
- 1/4 cup onion, minced

DIRECTIONS

1. In a mixing bowl, whisk together yogurt and mustard.
2. Add remaining ingredients and stir to combine.
3. Serve and enjoy.

NUTRITION

Calories: 405
Fat: 27.8 g
Carbohydrates: 17.5 g

Sugar: 4.6 g
Protein: 24.3 g
Cholesterol: 34 mg

153. Baked Dijon Salmon

PREPARATION TIME
10'

COOK TIME
10'

SERVING
6

INGREDIENTS

- 1 lb. salmon
- 3 tbsp. olive oil
- 1 tsp ginger, grated
- 2 tbsp. Dijon mustard
- 1 tsp pepper
- Salt

DIRECTIONS

1. In a small bowl, mix together oil, mustard, ginger, and pepper.
2. Preheat the oven to 400°F/200°C.
3. Spray a baking tray with cooking spray and set it aside.
4. Place salmon on a baking tray and spread the oil mixture over salmon evenly.
5. Bake salmon for 10 minutes.
6. Serve and enjoy.

NUTRITION

Calories: 165
Fat: 11.9 g
Carbohydrates: 0.7 g

Sugar: 0.1 g
Protein: 15 g
Cholesterol: 33 mg

154. Dijon Chicken Thighs

PREPARATION TIME
5'

COOK TIME
50'

SERVING
4

INGREDIENTS

- 1 1/2 lbs. chicken thighs, skinless and boneless
- 2 tbsp. Dijon mustard
- 1/4 cup French mustard
- 2 tsp olive oil

DIRECTIONS

1. Preheat the oven to 375°F/190°C.
2. In a mixing bowl, mix together olive oil, Dijon mustard, and French mustard.
3. Add chicken to the bowl and mix until chicken is well coated.
4. Arrange chicken in a baking dish and bake for 45–50 minutes.
5. Serve and enjoy.

NUTRITION

Calories: 348
Fat: 15.2 g
Carbohydrates: 0.4 g

Sugar: 0.1 g
Protein: 49.6 g
Cholesterol: 151 mg

155. Herb Pork Chops

PREPARATION TIME
10'

COOK TIME
1h 15'

SERVING
4

INGREDIENTS

- 4 pork chops, boneless
- 1/2 tsp dried sage
- 1/2 tsp dried parsley
- 2 tsp chives
- 1/2 cup chicken broth
- 1 tbsp. butter
- 1 tbsp. olive oil
- 1/4 tsp pepper
- 1/4 tsp salt

DIRECTIONS

1. Preheat the oven to 350°F/180°C.
2. Spray a baking dish with cooking spray and set it aside.
3. Season pork chops with pepper and salt and place in a prepared dish.
4. In a small bowl, mix together butter, oil, sage, parsley, and chives.
5. Rub butter mixture on top of each pork chops.
6. Add broth in the baking dish around the pork chops.
7. Cover with foil and bake for 1 hour.
8. Remove cover and bake for 15 minutes more.
9. Serve and enjoy.

NUTRITION

Calories: 317
Fat: 26.4 g
Carbohydrates: 0.3 g

Sugar: 0.1 g
Protein: 18.7 g
Cholesterol: 76 mg

156. Taco Chicken

PREPARATION TIME
5'

COOK TIME
6 hours

SERVING
4

INGREDIENTS

- 1 lb. chicken breasts, skinless and boneless
- 2 tbsp. taco seasoning
- 1 cup chicken broth

DIRECTIONS

1. Place chicken in the slow cooker.
2. Mix together chicken broth and taco seasoning and pour over chicken.
3. Cover and cook on low for 6 hours.
4. Shred chicken using a fork.
5. Serve and enjoy.

NUTRITION

Calories: 233
Fat: 8.7 g
Carbohydrates: 1.7 g

Sugar: 0.5 g
Protein: 34 g
Cholesterol: 101 mg

157. Broiled Fish Fillet

PREPARATION TIME
5'

COOK TIME
10'

SERVING
2

INGREDIENTS

- 2 cod fish fillets
- 1/8 tsp curry powder
- 2 tsp butter
- 1/4 tsp paprika
- 1/8 tsp pepper
- 1/8 tsp salt

DIRECTIONS

1. Preheat the broiler.
2. Spray broiler pan with cooking spray and set aside.
3. In a small bowl, mix together paprika, curry powder, pepper, and salt.
4. Coat fish fillet with paprika mixture and place on broiler pan.
5. Broil fish for 10–12 minutes.
6. Top with butter and serve.

NUTRITION

Calories: 224
Fat: 5.4 g
Carbohydrates: 0.3 g

Sugar: 0 g
Protein: 41.2 g
Cholesterol: 109 mg

158. Chicken Skewers

PREPARATION TIME
5'

COOK TIME
10'

SERVING
2

INGREDIENTS

- 1 lb. chicken breasts, skinless, boneless and cut into cubes
- 2 tbsp. fresh lemon juice
- 1 tbsp. fresh oregano, chopped
- 2 tbsp. olive oil
- 1/8 tsp cayenne pepper
- Pepper
- Salt

DIRECTIONS

1. Place chicken in a bowl.
2. Add reaming ingredients over chicken and mix well.
3. Place chicken in the refrigerator for 1 hour.
4. Heat grill over medium heat.
5. Spray grill with cooking spray.
6. Thread marinated chicken onto skewers.
7. Arrange skewers on the grill and grill until the chicken is cooked.
8. Serve and enjoy.

NUTRITION

Calories: 560
Fat: 31 g
Carbohydrates: 1.8 g

Sugar: 0.4 g
Protein: 66 g
Cholesterol: 200 mg

159. Grilled Chicken Breasts

PREPARATION TIME
10'

COOK TIME
15'

SERVING
4

INGREDIENTS

- 2 lbs. chicken breasts, halves
- 6 tbsp. fresh parsley, minced
- 6 tbsp. olive oil
- 1 1/2 tsp dried oregano
- 1 tsp paprika
- 1 tbsp. garlic, minced
- 6 tbsp. fresh lemon juice
- Pepper
- Salt

DIRECTIONS

1. Pierce chicken breasts using a fork. Season with pepper and salt.
2. Add lemon juice, oregano, paprika, garlic, parsley, and olive oil into the zip-lock bag.
3. Add chicken to the zip-lock bag.
4. Seal bag and shake well and place in the refrigerator for 1–2 hours.
5. Heat grill over medium-high heat.
6. Place marinated chicken on the grill and cook for 5–6 minutes on each side.
7. Serve and enjoy.

NUTRITION

Calories: 625
Fat: 38 g
Carbohydrates: 2 g

Sugar: 0.6 g
Protein: 65 g
Cholesterol: 200 mg

160. Chili Garlic Salmon

PREPARATION TIME
5'

COOK TIME
2'

SERVING
3

INGREDIENTS

- 1 lb. salmon fillet, cut into three pieces
- 1 tsp red chili powder
- 1 garlic clove, minced
- 1 tsp ground cumin
- Pepper
- Salt

DIRECTIONS

1. Pour 1 1/2 cups water into the instant pot and place trivet into the pot.
2. In a small bowl, mix together chili powder, garlic, cumin, pepper, and salt.
3. Rub salmon pieces with spice mixture and place on top of the trivet.
4. Seal the instant pot with a lid and cook on steam mode for 2 minutes.
5. Once done, release pressure using the quick-release method then open the lid.
6. Serve and enjoy.

NUTRITION

Calories: 205
Fat: 9 g
Carbohydrates: 1.1 g

Sugar: 0.1 g
Protein: 30 g
Cholesterol: 65 mg

161. Baked Lemon Tilapia

PREPARATION TIME
10'

COOK TIME
12'

SERVING
4

INGREDIENTS

- 4 tilapia fillets
- 2 tbsp. fresh lemon juice
- 1 tsp garlic, minced
- 1/4 cup olive oil
- 2 tbsp. fresh parsley, chopped
- 1 lemon zest
- Pepper
- Salt

DIRECTIONS

1. Preheat the oven to 425°F/220°C.
2. Spray a baking dish with cooking spray and set it aside.
3. In a small bowl, whisk together olive oil, lemon zest, lemon juice, and garlic.
4. Season fish fillets with pepper and salt and place them in the baking dish.
5. Pour olive oil mixture over fish fillets.
6. Bake fish fillets in the oven for 10–12 minutes.
7. Garnish with parsley and serve.

NUTRITION

Calories: 252
Fat: 14.7 g
Carbohydrates: 0.5 g

Sugar: 0.2 g
Protein: 32.2 g
Cholesterol: 85 mg

CHAPTER 9
Dessert and Snacks

162. Garlic Bread

PREPARATION TIME
5'

COOK TIME
5'

SERVING
2

INGREDIENTS

- ½ cup butter, melted
- Pinch salt
- 1 tablespoon fresh parsley, chopped
- 4 cloves garlic, roasted and minced
- 1 loaf French bread, sliced in half lengthwise

DIRECTIONS

1. Mix the butter, salt, parsley and garlic in a bowl.
2. Spread mixture on top of French bread.
3. Air fry at 400°F for 3 minutes.
4. Let cool for 2 minutes before serving.

NUTRITION

Calories: 312
Fat: 6g
Carbs: 18g

Protein: 9g
Sodium: 385g

163. Mozzarella Bites

PREPARATION TIME
5'

COOK TIME
5'

SERVING
4

INGREDIENTS

- 8 mozzarella sticks
- 2 tablespoons butter
- ¼ breadcrumbs

DIRECTIONS

1. Dip the mozzarella sticks in butter.
2. Dredge with breadcrumbs.
3. Arrange in the air fryer basket.
4. Cook at 320°F for 5 minutes, stirring once.

NUTRITION

Calories: 312
Fat: 6g
Carbs: 18,

Protein 9g
Sodium: 385g

164. Ranch Pretzels

PREPARATION TIME
5'

COOK TIME
5'

SERVING
4

INGREDIENTS

- 10 oz. pretzels
- 2 tablespoons olive oil
- 1 packet dry ranch seasoning mix

DIRECTIONS

1. Coat the pretzels with olive oil.
2. Sprinkle all sides with ranch seasoning.
3. Arrange the pretzels in the air fryer basket.
4. Cook at 320°F for 3 minutes.
5. Turn and cook for another 2 minutes.

NUTRITION

Calories: 312
Fat: 6g
Carbs: 18g

Protein: 9g
Sodium: 385g

165. Maple Barbecue Cashews

PREPARATION TIME
5'

COOK TIME
5'

SERVING
12

INGREDIENTS

- 2 tablespoons olive oil
- 2 teaspoons maple barbecue rub
- 1 cup raw cashews

DIRECTIONS

1. Blend olive oil and maple barbecue rub.
2. Coat cashews with this mixture.
3. Add to the air fryer basket.
4. Air fry at 370°F for 5 minutes, stirring once.

NUTRITION

Calories: 312
Fat: 6g
Carbs: 18g

Protein: 9g
Sodium: 385g

166. Pizza Bread

PREPARATION TIME
10'

COOK TIME
5'

SERVING
4

INGREDIENTS

- 1 cup marinara sauce
- 2 French bread, sliced in half lengthwise
- ½ cup mozzarella sauce, shredded
- 1 tablespoon fresh parsley, chopped
- 1 tablespoon fresh oregano, chopped

DIRECTIONS

1. Spread marina sauce on top of the bread.
2. Sprinkle the mozzarella cheese on top.
3. Add the chopped herbs on top.
4. Air fry at 400°F for 5 minutes.

NUTRITION

Calories: 312
Fat: 6g
Carbs: 18g

Protein: 9g
Sodium: 385g

167. Mexican Corn

PREPARATION TIME
5'

COOK TIME
10'

SERVING
4

INGREDIENTS

- 4 ears corn
- ¼ cup Cotija cheese, crumbled
- ¼ cup fresh cilantro, chopped
- ¼ teaspoon chili powder

DIRECTIONS

1. Add the corn to the air fryer basket.
2. Air fry at 390°F for 10 minutes.
3. Sprinkle with the Cotija cheese.
4. Cook for 5 more minutes.
5. Sprinkle with cilantro and chili powder.

NUTRITION

Calories: 312
Fat 6g
Carbs: 18g

Protein: 9g
Sodium: 385g

168. Smoky Chickpeas

PREPARATION TIME
5'

COOK TIME
18'

SERVING
4

INGREDIENTS

- 15 oz. chickpeas, rinsed and drained
- 1 tablespoon sunflower oil
- Salt to taste
- 2 tablespoons lemon juice
- ½ teaspoon ground cumin
- ¾ teaspoon smoked paprika
- ½ teaspoon granulated garlic

DIRECTIONS

1. Preheat your air fryer to 390°F.
2. Cook chickpeas for 15 minutes, shaking the basket once.
3. In a bowl, mix the oil, salt, lemon juice and spices.
4. Toss the chickpeas in the spice mixture.
5. Air fry at 360°F for 3 minutes.

NUTRITION

Calories: 312
Fat 6g
Carbs: 18g

Protein: 9g
Sodium: 385g

169. Potato Chips

PREPARATION TIME
5'

COOK TIME
15'

SERVING
4

INGREDIENTS

- Cooking spray
- 1 potato, sliced thinly
- Salt to taste

DIRECTIONS

1. Spray your air fryer basket with oil.
2. Spray the potato slices with oil.
3. Sprinkle potato with salt.
4. Air fry at 450°F for 15 minutes, stirring once or twice.

NUTRITION

Calories: 312
Fat: 6g
Carbs: 18g

Protein: 9g
Sodium: 385g

170. Roasted Macadamia

PREPARATION TIME
5'

COOK TIME
10'

SERVING
4

INGREDIENTS

- 1 lb. macadamia nuts
- Salt to taste

DIRECTIONS

1. Spread the macadamia nuts in the air fryer basket.
2. Cook at 250°F for 10 minutes, shaking the basket halfway through.
3. Sprinkle with salt.

NUTRITION

Calories: 312
Fat: 6g
Carbs: 18g

Protein: 9g
Sodium: 385g

171. Apricot Brie Snack

PREPARATION TIME
10'

COOK TIME
5'

SERVING
8

INGREDIENTS

- 1 package crescent dough sheets
- 4 oz. brie cheese, sliced
- ½ cup apricot preserves

DIRECTIONS

1. Spread the crescent dough sheet on your kitchen table.
2. Press the sheet onto muffin cups.
3. Top with the cheese and apricot preserves.
4. Air fry at 340°F for 5 minutes.

NUTRITION

Calories: 312
Fat: 6g
Carbs: 18g

Protein: 9g
Sodium 385g

172. Garlic-Parmesan Cheesy Chips

PREPARATION TIME
2'

COOK TIME
27'

SERVING
12

INGREDIENTS

- ¼ cup shredded Parmesan cheese
- ¼ cup shredded sharp Cheddar cheese
- ¼ teaspoon garlic powder
- Dash salt

DIRECTIONS

1. Preheat the oven to 400°F. Line a large baking sheet with parchment paper.
2. In a medium mixing bowl, combine the Parmesan cheese, Cheddar cheese, garlic powder, and salt. Mix well.
3. Place 2 teaspoons of the cheese mixture about an inch or two apart on the baking sheet, making about 12 chips.
4. Bake for 5 to 7 minutes, or until the chips are golden brown around the edges.
5. Remove from the oven and let sit for 15 to 20 minutes, or until the chips start to crisp. Enjoy.

NUTRITION

Calories: 98   Carbohydrate: 1g   Sodium: 333mg
Protein: 8g   Fiber: 0g
Fat: 7g   Sugar: 0g

173. Cheesy Baked Radish Chips

PREPARATION TIME
5'

COOK TIME
40'

SERVING
1

INGREDIENTS

- 1 cup thinly sliced radishes (2 bunches radishes)
- 1 tablespoon extra-virgin olive oil
- 3 tablespoons nutritional yeast flakes
- ¼ teaspoon salt
- Dash freshly ground black pepper (optional)

DIRECTIONS

1. Preheat the oven to 375°F. Line a baking sheet with parchment paper.
2. Place the radishes into a small bowl and toss in the oil.
3. In a small cup, mix the nutritional yeast, salt, and pepper (if using).
4. Place the oil-coated radish slices onto the prepared baking sheet in a single layer and sprinkle the nutritional yeast mixture lightly onto each slice.
5. Bake for about 15 minutes, then flip the chips and bake for another 15 minutes. Remove crispy chips, then continue to bake any remaining chips for a few minutes more at a time, until crispy and golden brown.
6. Serve and enjoy alone or with your favorite low-carbohydrate dip.

NUTRITION

Calories: 99

Protein: 5g

Fat: 7g

Carbohydrates: 4g

Fiber: 2g

Sugar: 0g

Sodium: 313mg

174. Savory Cheese Biscuits

PREPARATION TIME
5'

COOK TIME
15'

SERVING
8

INGREDIENTS

- 1 cup almond flour
- ¼ cup shredded Parmesan cheese
- ¼ cup shredded Cheddar cheese
- 2 teaspoons baking powder
- 2 teaspoons garlic powder
- ½ teaspoon salt
- 2 large eggs

DIRECTIONS

1. Preheat the oven to 350°F. Line a large baking sheet with parchment paper and set it aside.
2. In a large bowl, add the almond flour, Parmesan cheese, Cheddar cheese, baking powder, garlic powder, and salt. Mix well. Add the eggs and combine.
3. Scoop a heaping tablespoon of the mixture onto the baking sheet. Using a spatula, flatten the batter slightly into about 2-inch circles. Repeat, placing biscuits about an inch apart. This should yield 8 small biscuits.
4. Bake for 15 minutes, or until the top of the biscuits is slightly golden brown. Serve warm.

NUTRITION

Calories: 275   Carbohydrates: 8g   Sodium: 447mg
Protein: 15g   Fiber: 3g
Fat: 23g   Sugar: 1g

175. Italian Herb Muffins

PREPARATION TIME
5'

COOK TIME
12'

SERVING
4

INGREDIENTS

- Nonstick cooking spray
- 8 tablespoons almond flour
- ¼ cup shredded Parmesan cheese
- 1 large egg
- 1 teaspoon garlic powder
- 1 teaspoon Italian seasoning
- 1 teaspoon baking powder
- ¼ teaspoon salt

DIRECTIONS

1. Preheat the oven to 350°F. Line a muffin pan with 4 cupcake liners and spray the liners with nonstick cooking spray.
2. In a large mixing bowl, combine the almond flour, Parmesan cheese, egg, garlic powder, Italian seasoning, baking powder, and salt. Mix well until fully incorporated.
3. Scoop heaping tablespoons of the mixture into the lined cups until all the batter is used.
4. Bake for 12 minutes or until golden brown on the tops. Enjoy warm.

NUTRITION

Calories: 128
Protein: 7g
Fat: 10g

Carbohydrates: 5g
Fiber: 2g
Sugar: 1g

Sodium: 217mg

176. Cheesy Cauliflower Tots

PREPARATION TIME
5'

COOK TIME
15'

SERVING
4

INGREDIENTS

- 1 cup cauliflower rice
- ½ cup almond flour
- ½ cup shredded mozzarella cheese
- 1 large egg
- 1 tablespoon cornstarch
- ¼ teaspoon salt

DIRECTIONS

1. Preheat the oven to 400°F. Line a large baking sheet with parchment paper and set it aside.
2. In a large mixing bowl, combine the cauliflower rice, almond flour, mozzarella cheese, egg, cornstarch, and salt. Mix well until fully incorporated.
3. Scoop heaping tablespoons of the mixture onto the baking sheet about an inch apart until all the batter is used. This recipe should make about 16 tots.
4. Bake for 13 to 15 minutes, until crispy and golden brown. Serve and enjoy.

NUTRITION

Calories: 152   Carbohydrates: 6g   Sodium: 253mg
Protein: 9g   Fiber: 2g
Fat: 11g   Sugar: 1g

177. Mozzarella Mushroom Caps

PREPARATION TIME
5'

COOK TIME
20'

SERVING
12

INGREDIENTS

- 12 white mushroom caps
- 4 ounces fresh mozzarella pearls
- 2 tablespoons almond flour
- 1 tablespoon whipped butter
- ½ teaspoon garlic powder
- Dash salt

DIRECTIONS

1. Preheat the oven to 350°F. Line a baking sheet with parchment paper.
2. Wash the mushrooms and carefully remove the cap from each one. Place the mushrooms onto the lined baking sheet.
3. Place about three mozzarella pearls (about 1 tablespoon) in each mushroom cap.
4. In a small bowl, mix the almond flour, whipped butter, garlic powder, and salt. Sprinkle the mixture on top of each mushroom cap.
5. Bake for about 20 minutes or until the cheese has melted. Enjoy warm.

NUTRITION

Calories: 117
Protein: 8g
Fat: 9g

Carbohydrates: 4g
Fiber: 1g
Sugar: 0.25g

Sodium: 141mg

178. Almond-Crusted Mozzarella Sticks

PREPARATION TIME
10'

COOK TIME
6'

SERVING
6

INGREDIENTS

- 1 tablespoon cornstarch
- 8 tablespoons almond flour
- ½ teaspoon Italian seasoning
- ¼ teaspoon salt

- 2 large eggs
- 6 (1-ounce) light mozzarella sticks
- 1 tablespoon extra-virgin olive oil

DIRECTIONS

1. Place the cornstarch on a small plate. On a separate small plate, mix the almond flour, Italian seasoning, and salt. Beat the eggs in a small bowl and place between the two plates.
2. Cut the mozzarella sticks in half. Lightly coat each mozzarella stick in cornstarch, then dip and coat in the egg, and then coat well in the almond flour mixture. Coat each mozzarella piece well with the batter to enclose the cheese in the mixture so it doesn't spread onto the baking sheet while baking. Place each coated mozzarella piece on a large plate. Repeat until all the mozzarella pieces are coated.
3. Cover the plate with plastic wrap and place the mozzarella sticks in the freezer for about 2 hours.
4. Preheat the oven to 400°F. Line a baking sheet with parchment paper.
5. Place the mozzarella pieces about 1-inch apart on the baking sheet. Using a basting brush, coat each side of each mozzarella piece lightly with the oil.
6. Bake for 4 to 6 minutes, until the cheese starts to bubble, and the crust starts to turn slightly golden. Watch closely to make sure the cheese does not start to spread. Enjoy warm.

NUTRITION

Calories: 182
Protein: 11g
Fat: 15g

Carbohydrates: 4g
Fiber: 1g
Sugar: 1g

Sodium: 311mg

179. Almond Light-as-Air Cookies

PREPARATION TIME
5'

COOK TIME
10'

SERVING
8

INGREDIENTS

- 8 tablespoons almond flour
- 1 tablespoon low-sugar vanilla whey protein powder
- 1 tablespoon whipped butter
- 2 teaspoons vanilla extract
- 1 teaspoon baking powder
- 1 teaspoon finely granulated pure cane sugar
- ½ teaspoon stevia or no-calorie sweetener
- ¼ teaspoon salt

DIRECTIONS

1. Preheat the oven to 350°F. Line a large baking sheet with parchment paper.
2. In a large bowl, combine the almond flour, protein powder, whipped butter, vanilla extract, baking powder, sugar, stevia, and salt and mix well until fully incorporated.
3. Scoop heaping tablespoons of the mixture onto the baking sheet about an inch apart. Using a spatula, flatten the batter slightly into about 2-inch circles. This should yield 8 cookies.
4. Bake for 7 to 9 minutes, or until the edges of cookies are slightly golden brown. Keep a close eye on the cookies since as soon as this happens, you will want to remove the cookies from the oven to prevent overcooking.
5. Allow the cookies to cool slightly before serving.

NUTRITION

Calories: 117
Protein: 6g
Fat: 9g

Carbohydrates: 5g
Fiber: 2g
Sugar: 2g

Sodium: 288mg

180. Strawberry Gelatin Tea

PREPARATION TIME
5'

COOK TIME
5'

SERVING
1

INGREDIENTS

- ½ cup frozen sliced strawberries
- ¼ teaspoon stevia or no-calorie sweetener
- ½ cup hot water
- 2 tablespoons plain gelatin powder

DIRECTIONS

1. In a small saucepan, cook the strawberries over medium heat for 3 minutes, stirring frequently, until softened.
2. Stir in the stevia. Remove the pan from the heat and set aside.
3. Pour the hot water into a mug. Mix in the gelatin powder a bit at a time while continuously stirring with a fork. Keep stirring as you add in the cooked strawberries.
4. Blend the mixture in a blender for about 30 seconds, until frothy.
5. Pour into a mug. Sip once cooled and enjoy as a tea within about 15 minutes or so before it starts to set.

NUTRITION

Calories: 89
Protein: 12g
Fat: 0g

Carbohydrates: 10g
Fiber: 2g
Sugar: 5g

Sodium: 47mg

181. Subtly Sweet Coconut Milk "Flan"

PREPARATION TIME
5'

COOK TIME
5'

SERVING
1

INGREDIENTS

- ½ cup light unsweetened coconut milk
- 2 teaspoons vanilla extract
- 1 teaspoon stevia or no-calorie sweetener
- 1 tablespoon (1 packet) plain gelatin powder

DIRECTIONS

1. In a small saucepan, heat the coconut milk for 1 to 2 minutes, then sprinkle in the vanilla extract and stevia and stir to dissolve.
2. Sprinkle in the gelatin while stirring constantly to dissolve the gelatin completely. Remove from the heat.
3. Transfer the mixture to a blender and blend for about 30 seconds or so, until frothy. Pour into a small jar or mug.
4. Allow the dessert to set in the refrigerator for about an hour to firm.
5. Serve and enjoy.

NUTRITION

Calories: 130

Protein: 6g

Fat: 7g

Carbohydrates: 5g

Fiber: 0g

Sugar: 3g

Sodium: 51mg

182. Chia Chocolate Pudding

PREPARATION TIME
5′

COOK TIME
2 hours

SERVING
1

INGREDIENTS

- ½ cup unsweetened almond milk
- ½ cup nonfat plain Greek yogurt
- 2 tablespoons chia seeds
- 1 tablespoon vanilla whey protein
- 1 teaspoon unsweetened cocoa powder
- ½ teaspoon stevia or no-calorie sweetener

DIRECTIONS

1. In a canning jar, combine the almond milk, yogurt, chia seeds, whey protein, cocoa powder, and stevia.
2. Seal with lid and let sit in the refrigerator overnight.
3. Enjoy straight from the jar, or in a separate bowl if you are consuming a smaller serving.

NUTRITION

Calories: 257
Protein: 25g
Fat: 12g

Carbohydrates: 21g
Fiber: 11g
Sugar: 5g

Sodium: 122mg

183. Simply Vanilla Frozen Greek Yogurt

PREPARATION TIME
5'

COOK TIME
8 hours

SERVING
4

INGREDIENTS

- 4 cups nonfat plain Greek yogurt
- 4 tablespoons vanilla whey protein powder
- 4 tablespoons vanilla extract
- 4 teaspoons stevia or no-calorie sweetener

DIRECTIONS

1. In a large bowl or loaf pan, combine the yogurt, protein powder, vanilla extract, and stevia.
2. Cover and freeze overnight or for at least 8 hours.
3. About an hour before serving, set in the refrigerator to thaw slightly. Serve and enjoy.

NUTRITION

Calories: 183   Carbohydrates: 12g   Sodium: 96mg
Protein: 28g   Fiber: 1g
Fat: 1g   Sugar: 8g

184. Mashed Cauliflower

PREPARATION TIME
10'

COOK TIME
5'

SERVING
4

INGREDIENTS

- 1 large head cauliflower
- ¼ cup water
- ⬚ cup low-fat buttermilk
- 1 tablespoon minced garlic
- 1 tablespoon extra-virgin olive oil

DIRECTIONS

1. Break the cauliflower into small florets. Place in a large microwave-safe bowl with the water. Cover and microwave for about 5 minutes, or until the cauliflower is soft. Drain the water from the bowl.
2. Using a food processor, puree the buttermilk, cauliflower, garlic, and olive oil on medium speed until the cauliflower is smooth and creamy.
3. Serve immediately.

Ingredient tip: You can buy buttermilk in most supermarkets, but it's just as easy to make your own. Mix 1 teaspoon freshly squeezed lemon juice with 1/3 cup low-fat milk. Let the mixture sit for about 10 minutes, or until the milk begins to thicken.

Cooking tip: For even more flavor, microwave the cauliflower with chicken or vegetable broth instead of water and add ½ cup shredded Parmigiano-Reggiano cheese when you puree the mixture. You can add protein to this dish by blending in powdered egg whites or unflavored protein powder after the first puree (puree until smooth and creamy then add the protein powder and puree to incorporate).

NUTRITION

Calories: 62	Carbs: 8g	Sodium: 54mg
Total fat: 2g	Fiber: 3g	
Protein: 3g	Sugar: 3g	

185. Baked Zucchini Fries

PREPARATION TIME
15'

COOK TIME
30'

SERVING
6

INGREDIENTS

- 3 large zucchini
- 2 large eggs
- 1 cup whole-wheat bread crumbs
- ¼ cup shredded Parmigiano-Reggiano cheese
- 1 teaspoon garlic powder
- 1 teaspoon onion powder

DIRECTIONS

1. Preheat the oven to 425°F
2. Halve each zucchini lengthwise and continue slicing each piece into fries about ½ inch in diameter. You will have about 8 strips per zucchini.
3. In a small bowl, crack the eggs and beat lightly.
4. In a medium bowl, combine the bread crumbs, Parmigiano-Reggiano cheese, garlic powder, and onion powder.
5. One by one, dip each zucchini strip into the egg, then roll it in the bread crumb mixture. Place on the prepared baking sheet.
6. Roast for 30 minutes, stirring the fries halfway through. Zucchini fries are done when brown and crispy.
7. Serve immediately.

NUTRITION

Calories: 89
Total fat: 3g
Protein: 5g

Carbs: 10g
Fiber: 1g
Sugar: 3g

Sodium: 179mg

186. Pickle Roll-Ups

PREPARATION TIME
20'

COOK TIME
20'

SERVING
8

INGREDIENTS

- ¼ pound deli ham (nitrate-free), thinly sliced (about 8 slices)
- 8 ounces cheese, at room temperature
- 1 teaspoon dried dill
- 1 teaspoon onion powder
- 8 whole kosher dill pickle spears

DIRECTIONS

1. Get a large cutting board or clean counter space to assemble your roll-ups.
2. Lay the ham slices on the work surface and carefully spread on the cheese.
3. Season each lightly with the dill and onion powder.
4. Place an entire pickle on one end of the ham and carefully roll.
5. Slice each pickle roll-up into mini rounds about ½- to 1-inch wide.
6. Skew each with a toothpick for easier serving.

NUTRITION

Calories: 86
Total fat: 7g
Protein: 4g

Carbs: 4g
Fiber: 0 g
Sugar: 2g

Sodium: 540mg

187. Tomato, Basil and Cucumber Salad

PREPARATION TIME
15'

COOK TIME
30'

SERVING
6

INGREDIENTS

- 1 large cucumber, seeded and sliced
- 4 medium tomatoes, quartered
- 1 medium red onion, thinly sliced
- ½ cup chopped fresh basil
- 3 tablespoons red wine vinegar
- 1 tablespoon extra-virgin olive oil
- ½ teaspoon Dijon mustard
- ½ teaspoon freshly ground black pepper

DIRECTIONS

1. In a medium bowl, mix together the cucumber, tomatoes, red onion, and basil.
2. In a small bowl, whisk together the vinegar, olive oil, mustard, and pepper.
3. Pour the dressing over the vegetables, and gently stir until well combined.
4. Cover and chill for at least 30 minutes prior to serving.

NUTRITION

Calories: 72   Carbs: 8g   Sodium: 5mg
Total fat: 4g   Fiber: 1g
Protein: 1g   Sugar: 4g

188. Raspberry Sorbet

PREPARATION TIME
10'

COOK TIME
0

SERVING
2

INGREDIENTS

- 1 Tbsp Honey
- ¼ c coconut water
- 12 oz raspberries

DIRECTIONS

1. We need to take all of those ingredients that we listed above and add them inside a prepared blender. Blend until it is nice and smooth.
2. Pour this into a container and add the lid to the top. Add to the freezer to set for a few hours before serving.

NUTRITION

Calories: 131
Fat: 4g
Carbs: 8g

Protein: 6g
Sodium: 212g

189. Avocado Hummus

PREPARATION TIME
15′

COOK TIME
0

SERVING
2

INGREDIENTS

- 1 c edamame
- ½ c chopped avocado
- 1 Tbsp lemon juice
- 2 Tbsp olive oil
- ½ tsp minced garlic
- ½ tsp onion powder
- 1 tsp tahini

DIRECTIONS

1. Add all of these ingredients into a blender and blend to make smooth. Serve with some vegetables and enjoy it.

NUTRITION

Calories: 112
Fat: 4g
Carbs: 18g

Protein: 7g
Sodium: 126g

190. Avocado Detox Smoothie

PREPARATION TIME
10'

COOK TIME
30'

SERVING
2

INGREDIENTS

- ½ avocado, peeled and roughly chopped
- 1 banana, peeled and chopped
- Handful baby spinach, torn
- 1 tbsp. powdered stevia
- 1 tsp turmeric, ground
- 1 tbsp. flaxseed, ground
- 1 tbsp. goji berries

DIRECTIONS

1. Peel the avocado and cut it in half. Remove the pit and chop one half into small pieces. Wrap the other half in plastic foil and refrigerate for later.
2. Peel the banana and cut it into thin slices. Set aside.
3. Rinse the spinach thoroughly under cold running water using a colander. Chop into small pieces and set aside.
4. Now, combine avocado, banana, spinach, turmeric, flaxseed, and goji berries in a blender. Process until well combined.
5. Transfer to a serving glass and add few ice cubes.
6. Serve immediately.

NUTRITION

Calories: 221
Protein: 3.1g
Total Carbs: 28.6g

Dietary Fibers: 7.5g
Total Fat: 11.8g

191. Sweet Pumpkin Pudding

PREPARATION TIME
15'

COOK TIME
15'

SERVING
4

INGREDIENTS

- 1 lb. pumpkin, peeled and chopped into bite-sized pieces
- 2 tbsp. honey
- ½ cup cornstarch
- 4 cups pumpkin juice, unsweetened
- 1 tsp cinnamon, ground
- 3 cloves, freshly ground

DIRECTIONS

1. Peel and prepare the pumpkin. Scrape out seeds and chop them into bite-sized pieces. Set aside.
2. In a small bowl, combine pumpkin juice, honey, orange juice, cinnamon, and cornstarch.
3. Place the pumpkin chops in a large pot and pour the pumpkin juice mixture. Stir well and then finally add cloves. Stir until well incorporated and heat up until almost boiling. Reduce the heat to low and cook for about 15 minutes, or until the mixture thickens.
4. Remove from the heat and transfer to the bowls immediately. Set aside to cool completely and then refrigerate for 15 minutes before serving, or simply chill overnight.

NUTRITION

Calories: 232
Protein: 2.7g
Total Carbs: 56g

Dietary Fibers: 4.6g
Total Fat: 0.9g

192. Beet Spinach Salad

PREPARATION TIME
15-20'

COOK TIME
40'

SERVING
3

INGREDIENTS

- 2 medium-sized beets, trimmed and sliced
- 1 cup fresh spinach, chopped
- 2 spring onions, finely chopped
- 1 small green apple, cored and chopped
- 3 tbsp. olive oil
- 2 tbsp. fresh lime juice
- 1 tbsp. honey, raw
- 1 tsp apple cider vinegar
- 1 tsp salt

DIRECTIONS

1. Wash the beets and trim off the green parts. Set aside.
2. Wash the spinach thoroughly and drain. Cut into small pieces and set aside.
3. Wash the apple and cut lengthwise in half. Remove the core and cut into bite-sized pieces and set aside.
4. Wash the onions and cut them into small pieces. Set aside.
5. In a small bowl, combine olive oil, lime juice, honey, vinegar, and salt. Stir until well incorporated and set aside to allow flavors to meld.
6. Place the beets in a deep pot. Pour enough water to cover and cook for about 40 minutes, or until tender. Remove the skin and slice. Set aside.
7. In a large salad bowl, combine beets, spinach, spring onions, and apple. Stir well until combined and drizzle with previously prepared dressing. Give it a good final stir and serve immediately.

NUTRITION

Calories: 215
Protein: 1.8g
Total Carbs: 23.8g

Dietary Fibers: 3.6g
Total Fat: 14.3g

193. Grilled Avocado in Curry Sauce

PREPARATION TIME
15'

COOK TIME
25-30'

SERVING
2

INGREDIENTS

- 1 large avocado, chopped
- ¼ cup water
- 1 tbsp. curry, ground
- 2 tbsp. olive oil
- 1 tsp soy sauce
- 1 tsp fresh parsley, finely chopped
- ¼ tsp red pepper flakes
- ¼ tsp sea salt

DIRECTIONS

1. Peel the avocado and cut lengthwise in half. Remove the pit and cut the remaining avocado into small chunks. Set aside.
2. Heat up the olive oil in a large saucepan over a medium-high temperature.
3. In a small bowl, combine ground curry, soy sauce, parsley, red pepper and sea salt. Add water and cook for about 5 minutes, stirring occasionally.
4. Add chopped avocado, stir well and cook for 3 more minutes, or until all the liquid evaporates. Turn off the heat and cover. Let it stand for about 15–20 minutes before serving.

NUTRITION

Calories: 338
Protein: 2.5g
Total Carbs: 10.8g

Dietary Fibers: 7.9g
Total Fat: 34.1g

194. Broccoli Cauliflower Puree

PREPARATION TIME
10-15'

COOK TIME
15-20'

SERVING
2

INGREDIENTS

- 2 cups fresh broccoli chopped
- 2 cups fresh cauliflower, chopped
- ½ cup skim milk
- ½ tsp salt
- ½ tsp Italian seasoning
- ¼ tsp cumin, ground
- 1 tbsp. fresh parsley, finely chopped
- 1 tbsp. olive oil
- 1 tsp dry mint, ground

DIRECTIONS

1. Wash and roughly chop the cauliflower. Place it in a deep pot and add a pinch of salt. Cook for about 15–20 minutes. When done, drain and transfer it to a food processor. Set aside.
2. Wash the broccoli and chop into bite-sized pieces. Add it to the food processor along with milk, salt, Italian seasoning, cumin, parsley, and mint. Gradually add olive oil and blend until nicely pureed.
3. Serve with some fresh carrots and celery.

NUTRITION

Calories: 138
Protein: 6.1g
Total Carbs: 12.7g

Dietary Fibers: 4.6g
Total Fat: 7.5g

195. Peanut butter joy cookies

PREPARATION TIME
30'

COOK TIME
45'

SERVING
3-4

INGREDIENTS

- 250 ml quick oats
- 250 ml peanut butter, unsweetened
- 250 ml Splenda 1 tsp vanilla
- 1/2 tsp cinnamon, dried 1 egg

DIRECTIONS

1. Pre-heat oven to 350°F.
2. Place the peanut butter and Splenda in a mixing bowl. Using a sturdy spoon or hand beaters, beat the two together until smooth. Add in the egg, keep mixing, then add the vanilla.
3. Last, add in the oats and cinnamon. Continue to mix until everything is nice smooth dough.
4. Scoop the dough out a by dessert spoon and using your hands, roll into balls. Place the balls on a cookie sheet and squish them gently down with a fork.
5. Place cookies in the oven for eight min until golden brown. Wait for them to cool before lifting off the pan.

NUTRITION

Calories: 338
Protein: 2.5g
Total Carbs: 10.8g

Dietary Fibers: 7.9g
Total Fat: 34.1g

196. Chocolate almond ginger mousse

PREPARATION TIME
10'

COOK TIME
30' + 4h cooling time

SERVING
5

INGREDIENTS

- 325 ml milk, skim & cold
- 1 instant pudding package, fat-free and sugar-free
- 250 ml cool whip lite, thawed out
- 1/4 tsp ginger, dried
- 1 tbsp. almonds, sliced

DIRECTIONS

1. Pour cold milk into a mixing bowl. Beating steadily with a wire whisk, add the pudding mix and dried ginger. Keep whisking for two min. Fold in the cool whip topping.
2. Spoon into five pudding cups, refrigerate until needed. Garnish with sliced almonds just before servings.

NUTRITION

Calories: 310

Carbohydrates: 21g

Protein: 3.9g

Fat: 26.4g

Saturated fat: 9.5g

Polyunsaturated fat: 16.9g

Sodium: 90mg

Fiber: 10.2g

Sugar: 7.1g

197. Bella's Apple Crisp

PREPARATION TIME
20'

COOK TIME
20'

SERVING
4

INGREDIENTS

- 4 apples, hard and crisp, cored and sliced
- 1/2 lemon
- 2 tbsp. water
- 2 tbsp. agave nectar or one tbsp. honey
- For toppings:
- 200 ml old-fashioned rolled oats
- 2 tbsp. butter, cold
- 1/2 tsp cinnamon
- 125 ml chopped walnuts

DIRECTIONS

1. Heat oven to 350°F.
2. Place sliced apples in the bottom of an eight-inch pie plate or square cake pan.
3. Drizzle the water, lemon juice, and syrup over the apples.
4. In a mixing bowl, stir together the oats and cinnamon. Use a pastry cutter or two knives to cut in the butter mixture until it resembles coarse breadcrumbs.
5. Stir in the chopped nuts.
6. Sprinkle the mixture over the apples covering them completely.
7. Cover pan with tin foil and slide into the middle of the oven for twenty min.
8. Remove tin foil from pan and continue to bake for another ten to fifteen min until topping is golden brown.

Option Serving: with a dab of fat-free, sugar-free ice cream.

NUTRITION

Calories: 424	Protein: 14.6g	Polyunsaturated	Sodium: 572mg
Carbohydrates: 74.3g	Fat: 9.4g	fat: 7.4g	Fiber: 11.3g
	Saturated fat: 2g	Cholesterol: 94mg	Sugar: 24.2g

198. Red Energy Wonders

PREPARATION TIME
15'

COOK TIME
15'

SERVING
5-6

INGREDIENTS

- 75 ml almond butter
- 325 ml coconut, shredded and divided into a 225 ml portion and a 100 ml portion
- 125 ml oats, rolled 125 ml of strawberries
- 125 ml almonds 4 dates, Medrol, pit-less

DIRECTIONS

1. Place the 225 portions of coconut and all the rest of the ingredients in a food processor. At high speed, process until smooth and fully mixed.
2. Pour the remaining coconut onto a plate. With a spoon, scoop out one tablespoon of the mixture and form a ball. Roll this ball around in the coconut, then place it on a plate lined with parchment paper. Repeat until all of the mixtures are used.
3. Place the plate in the fridge for at least two hours before servings. Keep energy wonders in an airtight container in the fridge.

NUTRITION

Calories: 191
Carbohydrates: 17.9g

Protein: 6.3g
Fat: 12g
Saturated fat: 5.4g

Polyunsaturated fat: 6.6g
Cholesterol: 7mg

Sodium: 101mg
Fiber: 2.8g
Sugar: 8.6g

199. Chocolate Protein Pudding Pops

PREPARATION TIME
5'

COOK TIME
10'

SERVING
4

INGREDIENTS

- 1 (3.9-ounce) package chocolate-flavored instant pudding
- 2 cups cold low-fat milk
- 2 scoops of chocolate protein powder

DIRECTIONS

1. In a medium bowl, whisk the pudding mix, milk, and protein powder for at least 2 min.
2. Spoon into ice pop molds or paper cups. Insert an ice pop stick into the center of each mold or cup.
3. Freeze for 4 hours, or until firm. Remove from the molds or cups before servings.

NUTRITION

Calories: 215
Total fat: 2g
Protein: 12g

Carbohydrates: 36g
Fiber: 0g
Sugar: 27g

Sodium: 480mg

200. Strawberry frozen yogurt

PREPARATION TIME
5'

COOK TIME
4 hours

SERVING
4

INGREDIENTS

- 2 tablespoons honey
- 1 cup low-fat, plain Greek yogurt
- 4 cups frozen strawberries
- 2 teaspoons vanilla extract
- 1 teaspoon freshly squeezed lemon juice

DIRECTIONS

1. In a food processor combine the yogurt, strawberries, honey, vanilla, and lemon juice. Pulse until crumbly, then process until the mixture becomes creamy.
2. Transfer to a standard-size loaf pan. Cover and freeze for 2 hours, or until frozen but still soft enough to scoop, and serve.
3. Ingredient Tip: Berries are a great source of fiber and antioxidants and a wonderful addition to your diet. Switch it up and try this recipe with raspberries, blueberries, cranberries, or whatever you find in season and available.

NUTRITION

Calories: 135   Carbohydrates: 25g   Sodium: 39mg.
Total fat: 1g   Fiber: 3g
Protein: 6g   Sugar: 17g

201. Lemon mousse

PREPARATION TIME
15'

COOK TIME
4h 15'

SERVING
4

INGREDIENTS

- 1½ cups boiling water
- 1 (6-ounce) package sugar-free lemon-flavored gelatin
- 2 cups ice cubes 1½ cups whipped topping
- Fresh fruit, for serving (optional)

DIRECTIONS

1. In a large bowl, combine the boiling water and gelatin. Stir for at least 2 min, or until the gelatin is completely dissolved. Add the ice cubes, and stir until melted. Refrigerate until thickened, 5 to 10 min.
2. Fold in the whipped topping. Divide into four portions and refrigerate until firm, about 4 hours.
3. Garnish with fresh fruit before serving (if desired).

NUTRITION

Calories: 85   Carbohydrates: 6g   Sodium: 45mg.
Total fat: 6g   Fiber: 0g
Protein: 1g   Sugar: 3g

202. Mozzarella Balls Recipe

PREPARATION TIME
10'

COOK TIME
5'

SERVING
8

INGREDIENTS

- 1 package string cheese
- 2 cups Panko Bread Crumbs
- 2 tsp Italian seasoning
- 1 tsp parsley
- 1 cup milk
- 1 cup flour
- Marinara Sauce (homemade or store-bought)
- Oil for frying

DIRECTIONS

1. Split 1-inch pieces of string cheese
2. In a bowl by pouring milk and setting it aside, prepare the coating form. Put 1 cup of flour in a plastic bag and add 2 cups of panko, mixed with seasonings, into another bag.
3. Place the cheese, one handful at a time, in the milk.
4. Toss it in your bag of flour and shake well.
5. Put the cheese back in your bowl of milk, then coat it fully.
6. Toss and shake in the panko bag until uniformly covered.
7. Place bites of mozzarella on a plate or in a bag and freeze for a minimum of 2 hours.
8. Heat oil on medium heat. Fry until golden brown in hot oil. Be sure to take out them of the oil until they get too hot, or from the breading, the cheese will ooze.
9. With marinara sauce, serve soft. ENJOY!

NUTRITION

Fat: 1g

Potassium: 92mg

Fiber: 1g

Vitamin A: 55IU

Cholesterol: 3mg

Carbohydrates: 24g

Sugar: 2g

Calcium: 71mg

Sodium: 124mg

Protein: 4g

Iron: 1.6mg

203. Chocolate Protein Balls

PREPARATION TIME
40'

COOK TIME
0'

SERVING
10

INGREDIENTS

- 1 cup rolled oats
- ½ cup natural peanut butter
- 1/3 cup honey
- ¼ cup chopped dark chocolate
- 2 tbsp. flax seeds
- 2 tbsp. chia seeds
- 1 tbsp. chocolate-flavored protein powder, or as need

DIRECTIONS

1. In a bowl, whisk together the oats, peanut butter, honey, chocolate, flax seeds, chia seeds and protein powder until mixed evenly. Cover the plastic wrap with a bowl and refrigerate for 30 minutes.
2. Scoop the balls into a chilled mixture. Keep it cold before you serve.

NUTRITION

Calories: 188
Protein: 5.8g 12% DV
Carbohydrates: 21.5g 7% DV

Fat: 9.9g 15% DV
Cholesterol: 0.2mg
Sodium: 67.5mg 3% DV.

204. Instant Frozen Berry Yogurt

PREPARATION TIME
2'

COOK TIME
0'

SERVING
4

INGREDIENTS

- 250g frozen mixed berry
- 250g Greek yogurt
- 1 tbsp. honey

DIRECTIONS

1. In a food processor, mix the berries, yogurt, and honey or agave syrup for 20 seconds, until the ice cream texture is smooth.
2. Scoop and serve in bowls.

NUTRITION

Calories: 70
Fat: 0g
Carbs: 10g

Sugars: 10g
Fiber: 2g
Protein: 7g

Low in salt: 0.1g

205. Chocolate Avocado Pudding

PREPARATION TIME
40'

COOK TIME
0'

SERVING
4

INGREDIENTS

- 2 large avocados—peeled, pitted, and cubed
- ½ cup unsweetened cocoa powder
- ½ cup brown sugar
- 1/3 cup coconut milk
- 2 tsp vanilla extract
- 1 pinch ground cinnamon

DIRECTIONS

1. In a blender, mix the avocado, cocoa powder, brown sugar, coconut milk, vanilla extract, and cinnamon until soft.
2. Refrigerate the pudding for about 30 minutes until it is chilled

NUTRITION

Calories: 400
Protein: 5.4g 11% DV
Carbohydrates: 45.9g 15% DV

Fat: 26.3g 41% DV
Sodium: 22.6mg 1% DV.

CONCLUSION

Choosing to switch to a weight-loss plan can be difficult. But, if you have chosen the gastric sleeve surgery, then it's essential that you know how to eat after this surgery. Eating the right foods will help you on your way not only in losing weight but also in feeling better. This cookbook is for anyone who has undergone gastric sleeve bariatric surgery and wants to enjoy food while losing weight; without medication, diet pills, or any other type of drugs. In this cookbook are over 100 delicious recipes that are surprisingly easy and quick enough for a busy lifestyle.

Thousands of people are going through this difficult surgery and many of them come out with no weight loss. By knowing how to eat after gastric sleeve surgery, you will be able to eat in a healthier way and still lose weight. You'll save money, and I promise you that you'll have more energy, better moods, and feel better overall.

This is a book that can help you lose weight by eating the right foods in a healthy way. So if you are thinking about this surgery or have already had it done, please read this cookbook now.

If you are thinking about gastric sleeve bariatric surgery, then this is the cookbook you need. It's full of delicious recipes that are healthy, low in calories and low in carbohydrates. Get no more than 50 grams of carbohydrates per day, because you must stay lean. If you don't stay lean, then it's not a good idea to lose weight. This cookbook will help you lose weight but keep your lean body mass up.

"Eating right" for weight loss means consuming few calories and lots of nutrients. You must eat protein in order to keep lean, so be sure to include some meat with every meal. Any excess protein, however, will be converted into carbohydrates in your body.

This cookbook will also help you lose a lot of fat which is the most important step towards weight loss.

Fats are necessary for a healthy diet, but eating too much will slow down your weight loss progress considerably. If you are not losing weight as fast as you'd like, try this cookbook out and see how much fat is cut out of your diet.

Gastric sleeve bariatric surgery is a great way to get your eating habits fixed and your weight loss started in the right direction. It's still up to you, however, if you want to succeed. This cookbook is here to help you fix your eating habits and lose weight effectively.

This cookbook can help those who have had problems with losing weight, like binge eating or emotional eating.

The recipes in this cookbook will help you repair your relationship with food and lose the excess weight that has been bothering you for so long.

You are about to learn how easy it is to eat a healthy diet of lean protein, healthy fats, lots of vegetables and fruits and still lose weight. By switching your eating habits around with the recipes in this cookbook, you will finally begin losing weight and feeling better overall.

With the loss of all that excess fat, you will not only look better but feel better too. Your blood pressure may even lower and you'll be able to eliminate a lot of stress as well as unwanted pounds from your life.

This cookbook is very easy to follow and you can start eating healthy today.

Made in the USA
Middletown, DE
02 July 2021